MANDALIVE

mandala art therapy for working with emotions and behaviors

Embrace all of who you are

Work with both positive and negative parts of your personality
to access mental energy, creativity and new possibilities.

Lubica Hamarova, Pavol Rozloznik, Dana Dubravska

Concept and text © 2016 by Ľubica Hamarová, Dana Dúbravská
Illustrations © 2016 by Pavol Rozložník
Originally published in 2016 by Vydavateľstvo SLOVART, spol. s r. o., Slovakia
Translation © Dana Dúbravská, 2020
Editing by Melanie Votaw
Original Slovak title **Mandaly pre lepší život**

Copyright © for English edition KOMUNIKÁCIA s r. o. Slovakia, 2020

ISBN 978-80-973521-0-3

www.mandalive.com
www.komunikacia.sk

Table of Contents

We dedicate this book to our beloved friend and colleague Pavol,
who, apart from being an internationally acclaimed graphic designer
and a Zen monk, dedicated his life to creating the special therapeutic mandalas
included in this book.

We miss him very much, and as a gesture of memory and honour,
we would like to spread his great work around the world, so it can help people
on their inner journey of self-discovery.

What is the Color of Grief?

One night in a dream, I stood at the shore of an ocean. A monk approached me, and without saying a word, he drew a circle in the sand. He divided the circle into 12 pieces and created a star in the middle. Then, he told me to bring him the first thing that the ocean waves drifted to shore. The first wave brought a starfish, and the monk told me to put it in the middle of the circle where he had drawn the star. The starfish fell into tiny pieces and disappeared, but it left a red color in its place. The color filled the star.

Then, the monk told me to bring the next item that the ocean drifted toward shore. The second wave brought a seashell. I placed it inside the circle, and a yellow color came out of it, filling another part of the circle. I continued to bring items from the ocean, and all of those sea shapes changed into colors until all 12 parts of the circle were colored in.

The circle was beautiful, and it made me feel very good. It was somehow comforting to take the articles from the ocean and color the inner shapes of the circle with them.

When the full circle was colored, the monk asked me, "Do you know what this is?"
>"No, I don't."
>"Take a better look. This is your grief." Astonished, I looked at him and then again at the circle.
>"This circle full of colors is my grief?" I asked.
>"Yes," he nodded. "Those are the colors of your sad soul."

I had felt a deep sadness from the loss of my father. Four years before, I also unexpectedly lost my brother in a car accident. The grief was drilling into my bones, swallowing me up. My days and nights were heavy, and I couldn't see an end to it anywhere in sight.

>"What do you feel when you look at your grief?" the monk asked me.
>"Relief," I replied. "Huge relief. I feel like I'm finally able to breathe."

When I awoke the next morning, I still felt that strong sense of relief. It was soothing and liberating. After all those days of heaviness, I was finally feeling lighter. It was as if something heavy dropped off of me—something very heavy.

My experience was so strong and magical that I immediately wished others could experience the same liberating relief and calm. But what was I doing in that dream? How was it possible that I felt so relieved as a result?

After going over what happened to me in the dream, I realized that what I had actually done with the monk was color a mandala. The monk had designed a template for me for a "mandala of grief," and I brought colors into it. That mandala helped me work with my grief and experience my sadness in a different way. It allowed me to feel the emotion freely and easily and in a way that felt safe and secure.

Even before this dream, I was aware of the power of mandalas. I had colored them before. But this was something completely different. Never had I colored a mandala that represented a specific emotion, not to mention a negative emotion! My grief "showed its colors" through the mandala. "Would it be possible to do this with other emotions?" I wondered. And what about personal qualities or behaviors—both positive and negative ones? I was thunder-struck. "This is amazing!" I thought.

As a psychotherapist, workshop leader, and personal coach for many years, I taught my clients how to change their lives through work with their unconscious mind. This could be another great avenue for expressing emotions in a healthy way and embracing the contents of the unconscious mind called the "shadow."

But how could I create templates like the monk did in my dream?

The Birth of Mandalive®

Excited from all these inspiring thoughts running through my head, I thought of calling my friend and colleague, Pavol, who was a painter, graphic designer, and also a Zen monk.

   "Hi, Pavol. Do you think you could create a template for a mandala of grief?" There was a moment of silence on his end, and then, all of a sudden, he said, "I already see it!"

After a couple of days, Pavol presented me with the mandala of grief. He brought it together with a mandala of joy. They were both beyond beautiful. I started to use them right away in the next workshop I had with my clients. Gradually, we started to create mandalas of other emotions, qualities, and behaviors.

So this is how the mandalas of life, now called Mandalive®, were born. They were created from dreams to reality. They were born in order to help us see the invisible and accept the unacceptable. They were born to help us explore the secrets of our individual souls, to be able to touch the true self and experience a feeling of wholeness.

Together with Pavol and my daughter and colleague, Dana, we made the mandalas into a popular tool for increasing self-awareness and facilitating healing and growth through working with qualities, emotions, and behaviors. They've now been used by our clients for more than twelve years with great results.

We would like you to have the same extraordinary experience as our clients, expressing your emotions in a healthy way and meeting your own unconscious mind through the use of Mandalive®. We want you to have the chance to experience the magic of encountering what's normally invisible and untouchable.

Let Mandalive® help you better understand yourself and create a life that's more authentic, balanced, and fulfilling.

— Dr. Lubica Hamarova

Mandalas as a Tool
for Inner Self-exploration

What are Mandalas?

The word "mandala" comes from the Sanskrit and means circle, perimeter, and also center. Any circular image in nature or created by humans can be called a mandala. Circular images are the most common shape in nature. Molecules, cells, some shapes of plants, and some shapes of animals are also mandalas, as are the planets and galaxies. We all are inhabitants of a great mandala called the Earth.

The oldest depiction of mandalas is from the Ice Age, and mandalas have been found on all inhabited continents. The circle as a symbol of the sun, moon, and heaven depicted early gods and the perfection/flawlessness of nature.

The concept of a sacred circle can also be found in the architecture of ritual places with circular layouts like Stonehenge in Great Britain, as well as in layouts of cathedrals, rotundas, burial mounds, and church rose windows.

A labyrinth is a special large-scale mandala. We "color" it by walking, which means that as we walk, the totality of the body and soul come into harmony. Walking through the labyrinth, we become part of the mandala.

We can find mandalas mentioned in historical archives as visions of saints. During the Renaissance, Giordano Bruno used mandalas as a visualization tool. He believed that its perfect and balanced shape positively influenced the soul and helped people develop desired qualities and skills.

The circle of life can also be perceived as a mandala. It's a circle that starts with birth and ends with death. German author and therapist Rudiger Dahlke said that each of us encounters mandalas in our lifetime because we all carry them within us. We experience the mirroring of the mandalas within us every day, too. By perceiving and observing, we transfer experiences from the outside world into our inner world.

The circle is actually a symbol of expressing our inner experiences in the outside world. It enables us to renew balance and health. That's why indigenous peoples across the globe have used the symbol for healing.

We're in a continuous search for wholeness, harmony, safety, and deep inner peace. Dahlke explains that the mandala is able to facilitate the experience of centeredness, balance, and peace for us because this is its natural function.

Swiss psychiatrist Carl Gustav Jung, the founder of Analytical Psychology, suggested that the circle has a healing effect for the soul because according to old tradition, the soul has the shape of a circle. He considered the mandala to be an archetype and a component of the collective experience of all mankind. He thought of it as a symbol that we all carry within.

American psychologist Edward E. Edinger explained that children perceive human beings as a circular mandala structure, and the circle is also usually the first shape they learn to draw.

Suzanne Fincher, Jungian analyst and expert on mandalas, says that the unconscious is a moving force of our wholeness, and the mandala is a sacred space where we're able to experience wholeness. Mandalas contain and, at the same time, organize unconscious archetypal energies in a way that our unconscious mind is able to process. This means that the mandala enables us to safely meet with the energies of our unconscious and touch our wholeness. Fincher also says that mandalas enable us to reach into our unconscious sources of strength, development, and growth.

People who work with mandalas on an ongoing basis, as well as those who have researched its effects, report many benefits such as a relaxed mind, strengthened focus, calm, ability to deal with difficult situations, increased feeling of security and trust, and activation of inner potential. Working with mandalas, we're able to balance polarities within us and experience moments of true balance, harmony, and peace. It even helps us understand the meaning of life.

The Birth of Mandalive®

Mandalive® is a new approach in art therapy designed to increase self-awareness and facilitate healing and growth through work with emotions, qualities, and behaviors. It combines the benefits of coloring, mandalas, and shadow work in one unique tool. You tap into your potential on a completely new level by embracing all of who you are.

Mandalive® consists of uniquely designed mandala templates that are presented in pairs to represent opposite emotions, behaviors, or qualities, such as sadness/happiness or success/failure. By coloring the mandalas, you will learn to express your emotions in a healthy way and gain access to mental energy, creativity, and new possibilities that have—up until now—remained dormant in your unconscious mind.

Mandalive® mandala templates are available either in this book or as a mobile app. The advantage of the app is that you can print out the mandalas, which allows you to use the same mandala many times on different occasions. You can also color the mandalas digitally on your smartphone. The digital option has proven to be popular during commutes to work or when people have only a limited amount of time.

The mobile app is a live and growing database with new mandalas added continuously. You even have the option to suggest a new mandala that you would like us to create based on your particular needs.

Mandalive® is a truly innovative approach to inner work, self-exploration, and healing that will help you gain balance, energy, clarity, and confidence to live a more authentic and fulfilled life.

The author of this concept is Dr. Lubica Hamarova, a pioneer in applying the theories of C. G. Jung outside of psychotherapy and an expert on personal transformation, especially through working with the unconscious mind. She created this concept together with her colleagues, painter, graphic designer, and expert on mandala creation Pavol Rozloznik, and coach and trainer Dana Dubravska. Positive feedback from many satisfied clients who have used Mandalive® in workshops and coaching has made it a very popular tool for self-exploration and personal growth. Practitioners use this tool with their adult clients, as well as with children at elementary schools and/or special needs children, such as those with Down syndrome, ASD, or with intellectually gifted children and their parents.

When we color the specifically designed mandala templates of Mandalive®, we express our emotions in a healthy way and begin to communicate with our unconscious mind and its contents. According to Jung, the unconscious is the part of the psyche/mind where (besides other content) we store qualities, thoughts, feelings, or situations that we deem unacceptable or unwanted.

All that we don't want to have in our lives, all that we try to erase or ignore, doesn't just disappear. It "hides" in the unconscious mind. And these unwanted negative qualities, emotions, and behaviors are called the "shadow."

Mandalive® serves as a tool to help us get to know aspects of the shadow and make them conscious in a simple, friendly, yet very effective way.

Why is it Important to Express Emotions in a Healthy Way?

Most of us walk through our lives largely unaware of our emotions. We're so busy that we don't have time to explore how we feel during the course of the day. Or we actively suppress our feelings because they're unpleasant to feel, we're afraid we'll lose control of them, we think it's inappropriate to express them, or we're afraid to create conflict with others.

For example, you might suppress your hurt and anger when you receive negative feedback from your boss, or you might suppress your annoyance with a client. You may keep your disappointment to yourself about a friend who cancelled your night at the movies.

While there are situations in which it makes sense to keep our emotions in check, when we don't express them for a long period of time, we create tension, stress, anxiety, fear, insecurity[1]...and the shadow! It's like a snowball that gets bigger and bigger as it rolls down the hill.

In fact, the part of the brain that's associated with emotional processes—the amygdala—is then always "turned on" and contributes to chronic stress[2]. This is the part of the brain that's outside of our conscious control. So even when we engage in activities that would normally lead to relaxation, we can't fully relax, or the stress returns quickly.

During stress, our body produces specific types of stress hormones. While this is beneficial in short-term situations, high levels of these hormones that occur during chronic stress can interfere with learning and memory, increase weight gain, cause heart disease and blood pressure, increase the risk of mental illness and depression, lower immune function and bone density, and lower life expectancy[3].

On top of that, when we don't express our emotions in a healthy way, they become aspects of the shadow in our unconscious mind that look for alternative ways to express themselves. They might find an outlet through a different emotion. For example, anger might disguise itself as a fear, or an emotion might express itself as a different behavior. Suppressed fear could transform into anger and cause us to "act out" by criticizing others. Other times, unexpressed emotions express themselves through the body in conditions like allergies, rashes, stomach problems, or joint aches.

People who don't express their emotions on a habitual basis, or who only express emotions they deem to be socially acceptable, can easily lose their ability to experience life in a positive way. In other words, when we suppress negative emotions, we also inadvertently end up suppressing positive emotions such as joy, happiness, and a zest for life.

Therefore, it isn't just beneficial for us to express our emotions and talk about how we feel; it's crucial for our emotional and physical health. When we name and acknowledge our emotions, we relax the amygdala and activate the prefrontal lobe, which is the part of the brain that is more within our conscious control[4].

We develop our emotional expression habits in childhood. What habits did you create as a child? Stop for a moment and think about what you learned from your parents and other adults when you were growing up. Were they emotionally expressive? Were they vulnerable, or did they only express anger by losing their temper? As a result, do you allow yourself to feel and express the full range of your emotions, or do you tend to suppress them? If so, do you suppress all of them or only some of them?

As you go through your day, begin to observe yourself. Stop as you shower or drive somewhere and ask yourself, "What am I feeling right now?"

Why Work with Negative Qualities, Behaviors, and Emotions?

Throughout our lifetime, it isn't possible to suppress all of our negative qualities, behaviors, and emotions, while only expressing those we consider positive. Everything within the universe is created from polarities/polar opposites that—together—create unity. There are always two sides of a coin. On one side, we have darkness, and on the other, there is light. Joy complements sadness; cold complements warmth. We live the law of polarities in every moment of our lives.

Greek philosopher Heraclitos of Ephesus said that the movement in the universe is defined by polarities. The tension between them and their continuous movement guarantee that we live, change, and grow. Without polarities, we couldn't grow and move forward.

Human life is also created by uniting opposites. The egg that represents the feminine side accepts sperm that represents the masculine side. Oneness is created from two. We are born from the darkness of the womb to the light of life, so opposite polarities become an inseparable part of our life from its very beginning.

This also holds true within the psyche. It isn't possible to live only qualities, behaviors, and emotions that we consider positive, while repressing and ignoring their opposites. **If we repress negative qualities and emotions for a long period of time, they become part of the shadow in the unconscious, and this deprives us of access to their mental energy, which can actually be quite valuable.** We become exhausted, and we find it harder to achieve what we want.

When we have enough mental energy, we have more happiness, self-confidence, ability to focus, will, motivation, and productivity.

To live a balanced, fulfilling, and successful life and to use our potential to the fullest, we need the mental energy and positive aspects of all of our qualities, emotions, and behaviors. Yes, even the negative ones have positive aspects.

We simply can't divide all qualities, emotions, or behaviors into either positive or negative categories. Our psyches, and indeed the world, are much more complex than that. Emotions, qualities, and behaviors that we consider "bad" have their positive aspects and vice versa. It isn't always bad, for example, to be lazy, while it isn't always good to be hardworking.

Working hard is positive if we finish school or make a lot of money, but if we become workaholics, this behavior can cause us to destroy our health and relationships. Laziness is negative if we don't finish school or don't find a job. But if we need to rest, laziness might help us be healthier and better nurture our relationships.

Arrogance is bad if we yell at our children, but if we're able to realize its positive aspect and become more assertive and self-confident, it can be a good thing. It all depends on the situation. The same behavior might be beneficial in some situations while completely unhelpful in others.

So the true "life skill" isn't erasing what we judge as negative. The true life skill is to become aware in the present moment in order to determine which polarity is required. What's best in each specific situation? For example, should we speak up or remain quiet?

But nothing is inherently "good" or "bad." The true mastery of life involves recognizing that there are shades of grey, ambiguity, and complexity. Everything has both positive and negative aspects.

The qualities we consider negative and suppress for a long period of time don't stay in the unconscious without moving. Due to the law of polarities, the unconscious mind eventually brings our repressed shadow parts out into the open in covert ways. And the more we try to eliminate the negative qualities, behaviors, and emotions from our lives, the more our unconscious pushes them back into our conscious lives. So, what we repress and ignore will one day show up in a negative way. The shadow will force us to behave unpredictably and illogically, and in the worst case scenario, act in a way that's completely opposite from our values.

An example of shadow behavior is a loyal employee who suddenly steals money, a faithful wife who cheats on her husband, a responsible employee who misses an important meeting, or a patient mother who yells at her kids. We don't see the shadow directly, but in spite of our efforts to keep them at bay, they express themselves in our lives. They are our problems, illnesses, failures, setbacks, missed opportunities, and sufferings.

In other words, if we don't get to know the aspects of our shadow voluntarily, they'll eventually force us to deal with them whether we like it or not. That's why it's better to learn how to get to know them and bring them to consciousness voluntarily.

If we learn how to proactively "move" the aspects of our shadow from the unconscious mind to the conscious mind, they no longer pose a potential threat that could cause trouble in our lives. We can then restore the balance of polarities in our conscious world so that the unconscious mind doesn't have to do it in a compensating, potentially destructive way.

Our life is simpler and more balanced, and we have better access to our intuition. We're able to achieve our goals smoothly and easily.

Positive Shadow

The shadow in our unconscious consists of not only qualities we deem negative but also sometimes qualities and behaviors we consider positive. All of our abilities and possibilities that we have available but don't live out or express can, with time, become part of the shadow in our unconscious. The positive shadow represents our hidden possibilities and qualities that we would like to have but don't realize we already have. These positive aspects of the shadow are qualities that we admire or envy in others. For example, if we look up to Steve Jobs, our positive shadow quality might be creativity, success, or innovation.

It's important to activate positive aspects of the shadow because they represent our abilities, talents, and mental energies. They can help us achieve our goals. When our positive qualities stay repressed in the unconscious, and we don't live them out consciously, it's only their negative aspects that will eventually be available to us.

For example, if I envy someone for having discipline, and I don't express the positive aspects of discipline anywhere in my life, its negative aspect will increase in my life over time. I will start to have discipline in a compensatory manner. I might have "discipline" in overeating every evening or in breaking all promises I made to myself or to the people around me.

If we envy a quality in someone, it means we also have this possibility within us, but we aren't expressing it in our lives. If we wouldn't have the potential for it within us, we wouldn't be able to see it in others, and it wouldn't be "projected" from our unconscious into the outside world. Let's discuss how these projections occur.

Everything Around Us is a Mirror

Usually, we don't know what aspects of the shadow are in our unconscious until we look at our lives and the world around us with honesty and frankness. *The unconscious projects all of our shadow parts either onto people or situations around us. Usually, we find these people or situations unpleasant. In so doing, the unconscious mind "forces" us to open our eyes and realize something is out of balance.*

What does this look like in real life? For example, let's say you like discipline; you're hardworking and industrious. You nurture these qualities, you improve and develop them, and at the same time, you try to get rid of laziness and any lack of discipline in your character. You can avoid laziness and lack of discipline in yourself for some time, but you won't be able to permanently "erase" them from within yourself. They will become the shadow in your unconscious, where they'll remain for a while. But after some time, they'll start to "call for your attention."

First, they'll do this by projecting themselves onto people around you, so you'll start to notice more people as lazy and without discipline.

Projecting our shadow onto the world around us is a way for our unconscious to send us a "message" about their existence. It wants to inform us that we have an imbalance with regard to a certain quality, emotion, or behavior in our psyche. If we don't pay attention to these messages, we'll become lazy or lose discipline in some area of life where we expect it the least and where those behaviors will be the least beneficial. For example, let's say even though you care about your family, you still forget an important promise to your partner, or you don't hand in a project to your boss or client on time.

Mail from the Unconscious

Even though the messages from the unconscious are unpleasant, the unconscious mind means well. By projecting our shadow onto the world around us, it warns us that some quality, behavior, or emotion is out of balance. The unconscious always wants us to consider two options: ***Where do we live out or express this quality, behavior, or emotion without awareness in a way that is negative, or where are we missing its positive aspect?***

If your irresponsible colleagues at work irritate you, your unconscious might be trying to send you a message that you could be irresponsible somewhere in your life without realizing it. You might, for example, have been irresponsible toward yourself when you decided to start exercising but kept postponing it. Or maybe, you're lacking the positive aspect of irresponsibility somewhere in your conscious life by not being spontaneous enough when spending time with your kids.

While "decoding" messages from our unconscious mind that are projected onto the world around us, it's important to realize that the quality, emotion, or behavior we have in our own shadow is never completely identical to the quality, emotion, or behavior as we see it in others. Our unconscious communicates in symbols and metaphors, and it usually projects parts of the shadow onto other people in completely different ways. For example, let's say a person annoys you because he's too cheap to ever invite anyone for a coffee or lunch. This doesn't necessarily mean you've been stingy about money. You might have been stingy about giving praise to your employees or kids or in expressing love and emotions in your relationship.

The missing positive aspect that your unconscious wants you to notice might be that you should be "cheaper" or stingier about expressing your negative feelings. It's important to always look at different areas of your life in order to decipher the messages from the unconscious.

How to Prevent the Shadow from Complicating Your Life

If you don't want your unconscious to constantly point out your shadow aspects to you through annoying situations or force you to live the shadow out in an unpleasant way, you have to pay attention to them and make them conscious. You have to bring them from the darkness of the unconscious into the light of consciousness so that their compensatory expressions won't complicate your life.

We can identify our own shadow aspects by observing the world around us and by observing our reactions to the behaviors of other people. Our shadow parts are hidden in experiences and situations where we have a strong emotional reaction. Anger, envy, disappointment, sadness, shock, bewilderment, disgust, offense, as well as admiration and awe, are indicators that shadow aspects have been reflected onto the world around us. These emotions are a compass navigating us to find our shadow parts. The behaviors or qualities in others that we criticize, hate, detest, complain about, or gossip about are aspects of our negative shadow.

If we dislike people who are irresponsible, it's because irresponsibility is one of our shadow aspects. We try to nurture our responsibility and eliminate everything that we deem irresponsible. But remember that our own inner irresponsibility doesn't disappear. We simply push it away into our unconscious where it continues to live and grow. After a while, the unconscious decides to "notify" us of this repressed quality by projecting it onto others, and we react negatively when seeing irresponsibility in the people around us. If we weren't irresponsible in some area of life, for example, the unconscious would have nothing to project, and we wouldn't react emotionally to the irresponsible person.

Has a friend of yours ever reacted in a negative way to someone else's behavior, but you couldn't figure out why because the behavior didn't bother you? It's because that behavior was a shadow for your friend.

We can identify the shadow aspects that are projected onto the world around us by answering the following questions:

1. **What do I not like about this person/situation?**
2. **What makes me angry about this person/situation?**
3. **What do I envy about this person?**
4. **What do I admire about this person?**

If our colleague is lazy, but it doesn't bother us, it isn't an unconscious shadow part for us. If it annoys us, it's definitely an unconscious shadow part.

When we decipher the message from our unconscious by noticing the shadow quality, behavior, or emotion that has been projected onto others, we can explore it further. In order to make the shadow "conscious" and include it in our conscious world, we can answer some of these simple questions:

1. **Where in my life do I act like this, but I'm not able to see it? Where do I express this quality without realizing it? Where do I feel like this?**
2. **What is the positive aspect of this quality, emotion, or behavior? What could be its benefit?**
3. **What is the negative aspect of this quality, emotion, or behavior? What drawbacks can it have?**
4. **Where could I start expressing the positive aspect of this quality, emotion, or behavior in my life?**

By answering these questions, the shadow part "moves" from the unconscious into the conscious mind and ceases to be a threat for the future. It sees the light of the conscious world, and the unconscious no longer has to get our attention by projecting it onto people and situations around us.

Here's an example: It bothers me that my colleague slows down the entire team. The qualities that annoy me are: slow, slowing down others.

1. *Where in my life do I act like this, but I'm not able to see it? Where do I express this quality without realizing it? Where do I feel like this?* I'm slow when I make decisions in my private life, e.g. whether to go on a date with someone or not. I'm always slow in giving feedback to my friends on suggestions for our vacation plans together. I'm slow in losing weight.
2. *What is the positive aspect of this quality, emotion, or behavior? What could be its benefit?* Being slow is good if it helps me think something

over so that I don't make hasty decisions. It helps me be careful, and when I go on vacation, a slower pace gives me more enjoyment and rest.

3. *What is the negative aspect of this quality, emotion, or behavior? What drawbacks can it have?* Being slow is negative if I miss a meeting with an important client or if I don't seize some opportunity because of it.

4. *Where could I start expressing the positive aspect of this quality, emotion, or behavior in my life?* Maybe I lack slowness in the relationship I just started and shouldn't move in with my new partner after only three months together. Maybe I should "slow down" in being extremely forthcoming with my colleagues, who often take advantage of me.

Using Mandalive® to Prevent the Shadow from Complicating Your Life

Another effective way to prevent shadow aspects from complicating your life is to work with Mandalive®! Using these special mandalas, you'll be able to work with the contents of your unconscious that are normally inaccessible to you. As a result, you'll be able to "free" these qualities, behaviors, and emotions that are "locked up" in the depths of your unconscious mind. In a symbolic way, you'll be able to see and experience the shadow aspects that would otherwise be invisible. You'll see what your irresponsibility, poverty, sadness, failure, loneliness, pride, or self-confidence looks like on a symbolic level. You'll get to know their shapes and faces. They'll "show their colors" in full beauty within the mandala rather than show up in your life as a negative experience or sabotaging behavior.

Most of the time, we're afraid of things we can't see or imagine. But if we give the invisible energy a form, it becomes tangible and acceptable to us. We're able to see that we have nothing to fear, and we start the process of embracing the shadow.

By embracing aspects of our shadow, we neutralize their destructive energy and gain the positive mental energy that was hidden in the unconscious. Working with shadow emotions, qualities, or behaviors through mandalas returns us back to balance. We become open to changes, more authentic, more creative, and have better access to our intuition. We start to live our dreams, achieve our goals, and live in harmony with ourselves and those around us.

How to Work with Mandalas in This Book

Choosing a Mandala

How do you choose which mandala to work with? Perhaps you discovered a shadow aspect from the questions we mentioned previously, or you know of a particular emotion, quality, or behavior that you need to express. You can also close your eyes and open the book to a random page, or just look at the mandalas and pick one that attracts you based on its design rather than its name.

You can choose to work with just one particular mandala that interests you, or you can work with them in pairs. Either color the negative polarity followed by the positive one, or color each of them separately at different times.

What if you can't find a mandala in the book that's appropriate for the emotion or behavior you want to work on? In that case, go through the table of contents, and find the "next best thing." Many emotions are grouped in clusters, so if you feel furious or upset, you can work with the anger mandala. If you're experiencing grief, the closest mandala would be sadness. If you feel isolated, the loneliness mandala would work well for you.

Setting an Intention

The process of working with a mandala starts with an intention. Your intention is a map for your unconscious mind and increases the healing power of the mandala. You can use a general intention, or you can customize your own for a more powerful experience based on your specific needs.

General intention: I'm coloring this mandala to explore my _____ .
I open up to new opportunities and a new view of myself _____
and mandala, please, help me in access my full inner potential. Thank you.

Before you begin coloring, read this general intention given or write your own. At first, customizing your own intention might feel difficult, but with time and practice, you'll intuitively know what to write. It will help you to train your intuition and learn how to listen to your inner voice.

When writing the intention, you can either mention just the name of the emotion, quality, or behavior, or specifically write "anger at my friend," "anger at myself for failing to start exercising," "anger toward my company," etc. So the intention can look like one of these:

Intention: I'm coloring this mandala to express the anger I feel toward my husband. I let the colors and shapes of this mandala express and release my anger. Anger and mandala, please help me with this process. Thank you.

Intention: I'm dedicating this mandala to my sadness because my long-time friend isn't talking to me anymore. I let the shapes and colors of the mandala express and heal my sadness. Sadness and mandala, please help me with this process. Thank you.

Intention: I'm dedicating this mandala to the shame I feel about yelling at my kids. Let the coloring of this mandala help me release my shame and understand it better. Shame and mandala, please help me with this process. Thank you.

Intention: I'm coloring this mandala to express my fear of men. Let the shapes and colors of this mandala help me release and understand my fear. Thank you.

Intention: I'm coloring this mandala to express and release my stress as a result of the project I'm dealing with at work. Let the shapes and colors of this mandala release my stress. Thank you.

Working with a Negative Emotion, Quality, or Behavior

Stress and negative emotions that aren't fully expressed and released stay in our system too long and become toxic. Therefore, it's important to take the time to fully release them, and working with mandalas is a great way to do that.

You might want to release a negative emotion that you couldn't fully express because it was inappropriate in the moment, or maybe you didn't even realize you felt it until later.

If you had an experience that bothered you, but you aren't sure how you felt about it, the questions below can help. Ask yourself:

What did I feel in that particular situation?
What emotion was I not able to express?
What feelings stayed with me afterward?
How do I feel about the experience now?

Maybe the issue is less about an emotion and more about a behavior or quality that you expressed and wish you hadn't. If so, try answering the following questions in order to determine the best mandala for you:

How did I behave in this situation?
What quality or behavior did I express unintentionally? (This might be yelling at your kids or feeling afraid to speak up for yourself.)
What don't I like about myself with regard to this experience?

After you answer these questions, your mandala intention might look like one of these:

Failure
Intention: I'm dedicating this mandala to my failure to get the job at _____ _____ . Let the colors and shapes of this mandala help me accept my failure so that it doesn't enter my life in a negative way again. Failure and mandala, please help me with this process. Thank you.

Indecisiveness
Intention: I'm coloring this mandala to accept and understand my indecisiveness about _____ . Indecisiveness and mandala, please help me with this process. Thank you.

Fear
Intention: I'm dedicating this mandala to my fear of speaking up for myself. Let the colors and shapes of this mandala help me to begin to take better care of myself by speaking up on my own behalf. Fear and mandala, please help me with this process. Thank you.

If you're ill, you can also choose to color a mandala of sickness and dedicate it to your particular condition. You intention might be something like the following:

Intention: I'm dedicating this mandala to my diabetes [or whatever illness you have]. Let the shapes and colors of this mandala express and heal my diabetes. Sickness and mandala, please help me with this process. Thank you.

What if you want to embrace some negative emotion, quality, or behavior in order to have access to its positive aspects? For example, you might want to become positively "dependent" on a healthy diet or positively "alone" so that you can have time for yourself. The intention might look like one of the following:

Dependence
Intention: I'm coloring this mandala to get to know the positive aspects of dependency. Let the shapes and colors explore healthy dependency and attract it into my life. Dependence and mandala, please help me with this process. Thank you.

Mandala of Loneliness
Intention: I'm dedicating this mandala to being alone. Let the coloring of this mandala bring the healthy and positive aspects of being alone into my life. Aloneness and mandala, please help me with this process. Thank you.

Intention: I'm dedicating this mandala to the positive side of sadness. Let the shapes and colors of this mandala bring me understanding of the positive aspects of sadness. Sadness and mandala, please help me with this process. Thank you.

Working with a Positive Emotion, Quality, or Behavior

Just as you saw in the last group of intentions, we work with positive emotions, qualities, or behaviors because they're missing in our life. We want to cultivate more of them into our life in general, or we want to have more of them in a particular situation. For example, you might want to be happier with your family, more carefree in your new job, or have the courage to start a new business. Or you may just want to feel more courageous or content in general.

The intentions for those situations might look like one of these:

Happiness
Intention: I'm coloring this mandala to have/activate more happiness in my family life. Let the shapes and colors of this mandala bring me more happiness with my family. Happiness and mandala, please help me with this process. Thank you.

Carefreeness
Intention: I'm dedicating this mandala to feeling more carefree in my new job. Carefree feeling and mandala, please help me with this process. Thank you.

Courage
Intention: I'm coloring this mandala to support my courage to start a new business.

Let the shapes and colors of this mandala activate my courage to start a new business. Courage and mandala, please help me with this process. Thank you.

Wealth
Intention: I'm dedicating this mandala to activating more wealth in all areas of my life. Let the coloring of this mandala bring more wealth into every area of my life. Wealth and mandala, please help me with this process. Thank you.

Beginning and Ending Mandalas

There are two special mandalas in the book that will bring you support for beginnings and endings in your life, such as the beginning or end of a project, relationship, detox, etc. The intentions might look like one of the following:

Intention: I'm dedicating this mandala to the start of my new project _____ . Let the shapes and colors of this mandala support me as I start this project. Thank you.

Intention: I'm coloring this mandala to support the start of my new relationship with _____ . Beginning and mandala, please help me with this process. Thank you.

Intention: I'm dedicating this mandala to finishing my work project _____ . Let the shapes and colors of the mandala help me finish this project successfully. Thank you.

Intention: I'm coloring this mandala to finally end my unhealthy relationship with _____ . End and mandala, please help me with this process. Thank you.

Working with Mandalive® After You Read or Write Your Intention

After you've read or written your intention, follow this step-by-step process to work with your chosen mandala.

1. Please set aside enough time to color the Mandalive® template so that you can complete it in one sitting. Ideally, work with the mandala in a pleasant, clean, and peaceful environment without any music. There should be no drinks or food on the table while you color.

2. Color the mandalas using colored pencils, crayons, or felt pens. While coloring, respect the shapes within each mandala. You can connect the smaller shapes to form larger ones if you still use the shape defined within the mandala. However, please don't create new shapes that don't already exist within the mandalas, and don't color outside the lines. Color all of the shapes and areas of the mandala; it's best if you don't leave any area uncolored so that you can fully experience the powerful effect of all of the shapes, symbols, and colors. If you feel strongly about leaving some areas uncolored, please just color in more areas than you leave uncolored.

3. You can choose the colors consciously, or you can choose them intuitively with your eyes closed. You can select a set number of colors in advance and color the whole mandala only with them, or you can color each part of the mandala with different colors. It's up to you. Ideally, from time to time, change the way you pick the colors.

4. Color the mandalas of the qualities and emotions that you reject or find unpleasant by starting from the edges and working toward the center. When you color mandalas of positive qualities that are already in your consciousness, color from the center out toward the edges. This is a recommended, rather than a strict rule, however. You might want to color the same mandala twice in a row and try it both ways, first starting from the edges and moving toward the center, followed by the opposite.

5. You can keep the mandala for some time after you've colored it and even display it, if you like. After a period of time, you may choose to tear negative mandalas into pieces or burn them. Positive mandalas can serve as "amulets" or Feng Shui symbols and can be on long-term display somewhere in your house or office.

6. When coloring mandalas, you access the content of your unconscious mind. Therefore, you might experience various emotional states like anger, fear, hurt, stress, rejection, or disgust. Do your best to allow these feelings to flow freely from your unconscious so that you can express them safely within the mandala coloring process. If you release negative emotions in a safe way while working with the mandalas, you can prevent your unconscious from releasing them in

your life in a compensatory and destructive way. For example, if you express your anger or frustration while coloring a mandala, you won't overreact when your kids frustrate you, or you won't become upset and overly sensitive when your boss gives you feedback. That way, you will live a more balanced and ful-filled life.

Stories of Success with Mandalive®

Susan

Susan was starting her own business for the first time in her life. Before, she had always partnered with someone else, so this time, she had doubts about whether she could manage on her own. She even started to have nightmares, and every morning when she woke up, she felt stressed for no obvious reason. She decided to use Mandalive® mandalas to manage the situation.

First, she asked herself: How do I feel about starting my own business?

The answers that came into her mind were that she was scared she wouldn't be able to make enough money, that she wouldn't have enough courage to ap-proach new customers, and that she'd lose her savings, forcing her to close the business down. Based on these feelings, she identified these five mandala pairs to work with:

Worry – Carefreeness
Fear – Courage
Stress – Tranquillity
Poverty – Wealth
Failure – Success

She spent ten days coloring the mandalas—one for each day—using the follow-ing intentions:

1. Worry
   I'm coloring this mandala to express all of my worries about starting my new business. Let the shapes and colors of this mandala release my worries. Thank you.

2. Carefreeness

I'm dedicating this mandala to feeling more carefree about starting my new business on my own. Carefree feeling and mandala, please help me enjoy what I do. Thank you.

3. Fear

I'm coloring this mandala to express and accept all of my fears about starting a new business. Let the shapes and colors of this mandala help me let go of my fears. Thank you.

4. Courage

I dedicate this mandala to my courage in starting my new company and to help me easily face the challenges that will occur along the way. Courage and mandala, please help me with this process. Thank you.

5. Stress

I'm coloring this mandala to get out all the stress I feel about starting my new company on my own. Let the shapes and colors of this mandala help me get the stress out of my body and mind. Thank you.

6. Tranquility

I'm coloring this mandala to support my inner tranquility that will help me succeed in building my new company. Tranquility and mandala, please help me with this process. Thank you.

7. Poverty

I'm dedicating this mandala to accepting poverty and its gifts. Let the shapes and colors of this mandala help me find all of the positive aspects that poverty possesses. Thank you.

8. Wealth

I'm coloring this mandala to attract wealth into my newly started business. Let the shapes and colors help me activate wealth in my company. Thank you.

9. Failure

I'm coloring this mandala to explore and understand failure. Let the shapes and colors of this mandala help me find the gifts in failure. Failure and mandala, please help me with this process. Thank you.

10. Success

I'm dedicating this mandala to the success of my newly started business. Let the shapes and colors of this mandala express and attract success into my business life. Success and mandala, please help me with this process. Thank you.

After days of coloring the ten mandalas, Susan started to feel relieved and stopped having nightmares. She was able to perform her new business duties without so much anxiety, and she even acquired ten new customers shortly after.

Since then, when the doubts come back or she encounters an obstacle, Susan pauses, notices her feelings, and finds several mandalas to color to help her release the stressful feelings. In this way, she's able to stay focused and succeed in her business.

Kathy

Kathy was married for more than seven years when her husband came home from a business trip and announced that he wanted to separate from her. She hadn't been aware of any problems between them, so the news was a complete shock. She tried to talk about it with her husband, but he refused, saying he'd met someone else.

Kathy was devastated and went into a panic. She didn't even feel she could call her best friend or parents for help because she was so humiliated. She had used Mandalive® mandalas with her son to teach him how to express emotions in a healthy way, so she decided to try the mandalas again to help her deal with her intense emotions. She wrote down that she felt rejected, ashamed, and lonely. She also felt that the situation was unjust, so she worked with the "injustice" mandala.

The first two days, Kathy worked with the following mandalas, coloring two each day and writing down these intentions:

1. Injustice

I'm dedicating this mandala to my feeling of injustice about my husband's treatment of me in deciding to leave me and our son. Let the shapes and colors of this mandala help me understand and release this feeling of injustice in a healthy way. Injustice and mandala, please help me with this process. Thank you.

2. Rejection

I'm coloring this mandala to express and release my feelings of rejection. Let the shapes and colors of this mandala help me understand and heal these feelings. Rejection and mandala, please help me with this process. Thank you.

3. Shame

I'm dedicating this mandala to my feelings of shame that my husband is leaving me and that my marriage will be a failure. Let the shapes and colors of this mandala express and release this shame in a healthy way. Thank you.

4. Loneliness

I'm coloring this mandala to express my feelings of loneliness as a result of my husband leaving me. Let the shapes and colors of this mandala express and release this loneliness. Thank you.

Immediately after coloring the first mandala, Kathy felt relief, and her panicky heartbeat slowed down. With the second mandala, the fog in her head disappeared, and she was able to fall asleep. The next day, she colored the other two mandalas and gained enough courage and energy to call her best friend for emotional support.

After a couple of days, Kathy decided to write down her thoughts and feelings about her situation. This time, hatred, sadness, and insecurity about her future came to mind. So, she worked with the mandalas again, writing the following intentions before starting to color:

1. Hate

I'm coloring this mandala to express the hate I feel toward my husband because he found a lover and is now leaving me. Let the shapes and colors of this mandala help me understand this hate and release it in a healthy way. Hate and mandala, please help me with this process. Thank you.

2. Sadness

I'm dedicating this mandala to my sadness because my husband is leaving me, and my marriage is over. Sadness and mandala, please help me with this process. Thank you.

3. Insecurity

I'm dedicating this mandala to my insecurity about the future. Let the shapes and colors of this mandala help me understand and release this insecurity. Thank you.

After coloring these mandalas, Kathy felt relief again and was able to talk to her parents, who advised her to contact their family lawyer. They also suggested she see a therapist about how best to tell her son about the situation.

Peter

Peter hadn't been feeling well for several days, but instead of improving, his temperature began to rise. A doctor prescribed some medication that didn't work. In four days, he was scheduled to give a speech at a big conference, but he was afraid his illness would force him to cancel. The conference was very important for his company because they were launching a new project, and no one else knew enough to take his place.

Peter decided to try working with Mandalive®. First, he asked himself: How do I feel? How does feeling sick make me behave?

Here are the answers he wrote down: "I'm sick, angry, desperate, and I feel like I'm being controlled by some external force." Based on his answer, Peter chose to work with the following mandalas: Sickness, Anger, Despair, Hope, Health.

His intentions were:

1. Sickness
   I'm coloring this mandala to express and understand my sickness. Let the colors and shapes of this mandala take away my sickness. Sickness and mandala, please help me with this process. Thank you.

2. Anger
   I'm coloring this mandala to express and release my anger about being sick and maybe unable to give my speech at the conference. Let the shapes and colors of this mandala express and release my anger. Anger and mandala, please help me with this process. Thank you.

3. Despair
   I'm coloring this mandala to express my despair about being sick for a week without any significant improvement. Let the shapes and colors of this mandala help me understand and release this despair. Despair and mandala, please help me with this process. Thank you.

4. Hope
   I'm dedicating this mandala to my hope that I'll get well soon and be able to attend the conference that's very important for me. Let the shapes and colors of this mandala bring me hope. Hope and mandala, please help me with this process. Thank you.

5. Health

I'm dedicating this mandala to becoming healthy. Let the shapes and colors of this mandala support my health and energy. Health and mandala, please help me with this process. Thank you.

Over the next two days, Peter's temperature went down, and his condition finally started to improve. The day before the conference, he worked with the mandala of health and was able to give a successful speech after all!

It's Your Turn!

We hope that these explanations and examples have made you feel excited about trying Mandalive®. This kind of inner work is invaluable, and we believe you'll discover a tool that you'll want to use for the rest of your life to maintain greater peace within yourself and improved relationships with others.

If you want to use this tool regularly, you can buy the mobile app in either App store or Google Play. It has many great features, such as the "resonance" button that can show you which emotions or qualities are important for you on a given day. From the app, you can print as many mandala templates as you want using a wireless printer, or you can color them directly within the app. You can store them in your own library, share them on social media, or even "burn" them within the app. Go and see for yourself—the basic version with four mandalas of sadness/happiness and failure/success is free!

"I am not what happened to me,
I am what I choose to become."

Carl Gustav Jung

Mandalas for Coloring

ANGER

1. Where in my life do I act like this, but I'm not able to see it? Where do I express this quality without realizing it? Where do I feel like this?

_____

_____

_____

_____

_____

_____

2. What is the positive aspect of this quality, emotion, or behavior? What could be its benefit?

_____

_____

_____

_____

_____

3. What is the negative aspect of this quality, emotion, or behavior? What drawbacks can it have?

_____

_____

_____

_____

_____

4. Where could I start expressing the positive aspect of this quality, emotion, or behavior in my life?

_____

_____

_____

_____

_____

INTENTION:
_____
_____
_____
_____

CALMNESS

1. Where in my life do I act like this, but I'm not able to see it? Where do I express this quality without realizing it? Where do I feel like this?

_____

_____

_____

_____

_____

_____

2. What is the positive aspect of this quality, emotion, or behavior? What could be its benefit?

_____

_____

_____

_____

_____

_____

3. What is the negative aspect of this quality, emotion, or behavior? What drawbacks can it have?

_____

_____

_____

_____

_____

_____

4. Where could I start expressing the positive aspect of this quality, emotion, or behavior in my life?

_____

_____

_____

_____

_____

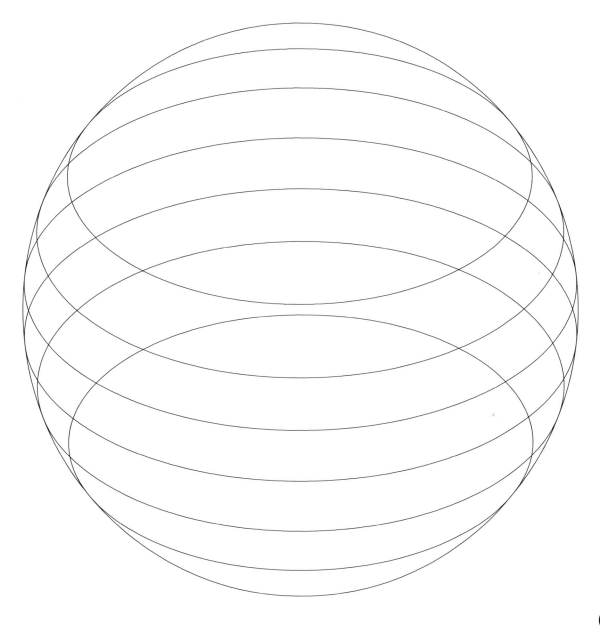

INTENTION:

FAILURE

1. Where in my life do I act like this, but I'm not able to see it? Where do I express this quality without realizing it? Where do I feel like this?

_____

_____

_____

_____

_____

_____

2. What is the positive aspect of this quality, emotion, or behavior? What could be its benefit?

_____

_____

_____

_____

_____

_____

3. What is the negative aspect of this quality, emotion, or behavior? What drawbacks can it have?

_____

_____

_____

_____

_____

_____

4. Where could I start expressing the positive aspect of this quality, emotion, or behavior in my life?

_____

_____

_____

_____

_____

_____

INTENTION:

SUCCESS

1. Where in my life do I act like this, but I'm not able to see it? Where do I express this quality without realizing it? Where do I feel like this?

_____

_____

_____

_____

_____

2. What is the positive aspect of this quality, emotion, or behavior? What could be its benefit?

_____

_____

_____

_____

_____

3. What is the negative aspect of this quality, emotion, or behavior? What drawbacks can it have?

_____

_____

_____

_____

_____

4. Where could I start expressing the positive aspect of this quality, emotion, or behavior in my life?

_____

_____

_____

_____

_____

INTENTION:

SADNESS

1. Where in my life do I act like this, but I'm not able to see it? Where do I express this quality without realizing it? Where do I feel like this?

_____

_____

_____

_____

_____

2. What is the positive aspect of this quality, emotion, or behavior? What could be its benefit?

_____

_____

_____

_____

_____

3. What is the negative aspect of this quality, emotion, or behavior? What drawbacks can it have?

_____

_____

_____

_____

_____

4. Where could I start expressing the positive aspect of this quality, emotion, or behavior in my life?

_____

_____

_____

_____

_____

INTENTION:

HAPPINESS

1. Where in my life do I act like this, but I'm not able to see it? Where do I express this quality without realizing it? Where do I feel like this?

_____

_____

_____

_____

_____

_____

2. What is the positive aspect of this quality, emotion, or behavior? What could be its benefit?

_____

_____

_____

_____

_____

3. What is the negative aspect of this quality, emotion, or behavior? What drawbacks can it have?

_____

_____

_____

_____

_____

4. Where could I start expressing the positive aspect of this quality, emotion, or behavior in my life?

_____

_____

_____

_____

_____

_____

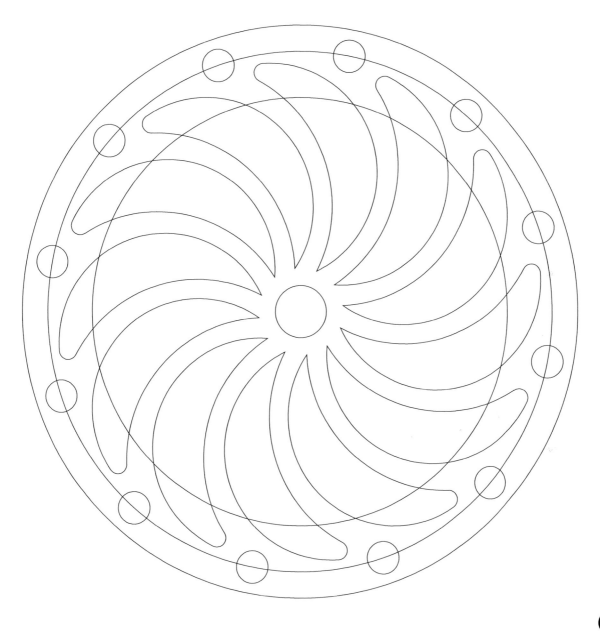

INTENTION:

SHAME

1. Where in my life do I act like this, but I'm not able to see it? Where do I express this quality without realizing it? Where do I feel like this?

_____

_____

_____

_____

_____

_____

2. What is the positive aspect of this quality, emotion, or behavior? What could be its benefit?

_____

_____

_____

_____

_____

_____

3. What is the negative aspect of this quality, emotion, or behavior? What drawbacks can it have?

_____

_____

_____

_____

_____

_____

4. Where could I start expressing the positive aspect of this quality, emotion, or behavior in my life?

_____

_____

_____

_____

_____

_____

INTENTION:

PRIDE

1. Where in my life do I act like this, but I'm not able to see it? Where do I express this quality without realizing it? Where do I feel like this?

_____

_____

_____

_____

_____

2. What is the positive aspect of this quality, emotion, or behavior? What could be its benefit?

_____

_____

_____

_____

_____

3. What is the negative aspect of this quality, emotion, or behavior? What drawbacks can it have?

_____

_____

_____

_____

_____

4. Where could I start expressing the positive aspect of this quality, emotion, or behavior in my life?

_____

_____

_____

_____

_____

INTENTION:

WORRY

1. Where in my life do I act like this, but I'm not able to see it? Where do I express this quality without realizing it? Where do I feel like this?

_____

_____

_____

_____

_____

_____

2. What is the positive aspect of this quality, emotion, or behavior? What could be its benefit?

_____

_____

_____

_____

_____

3. What is the negative aspect of this quality, emotion, or behavior? What drawbacks can it have?

_____

_____

_____

_____

_____

4. Where could I start expressing the positive aspect of this quality, emotion, or behavior in my life?

_____

_____

_____

_____

_____

INTENTION:

CAREFREENESS

1. Where in my life do I act like this, but I'm not able to see it? Where do I express this quality without realizing it? Where do I feel like this?

_____

_____

_____

_____

_____

_____

2. What is the positive aspect of this quality, emotion, or behavior? What could be its benefit?

_____

_____

_____

_____

_____

3. What is the negative aspect of this quality, emotion, or behavior? What drawbacks can it have?

_____

_____

_____

_____

_____

4. Where could I start expressing the positive aspect of this quality, emotion, or behavior in my life?

_____

_____

_____

_____

_____

INTENTION:

POVERTY

1. Where in my life do I act like this, but I'm not able to see it? Where do I express this quality without realizing it? Where do I feel like this?

_____

_____

_____

_____

_____

2. What is the positive aspect of this quality, emotion, or behavior? What could be its benefit?

_____

_____

_____

_____

_____

3. What is the negative aspect of this quality, emotion, or behavior? What drawbacks can it have?

_____

_____

_____

_____

_____

4. Where could I start expressing the positive aspect of this quality, emotion, or behavior in my life?

_____

_____

_____

_____

_____

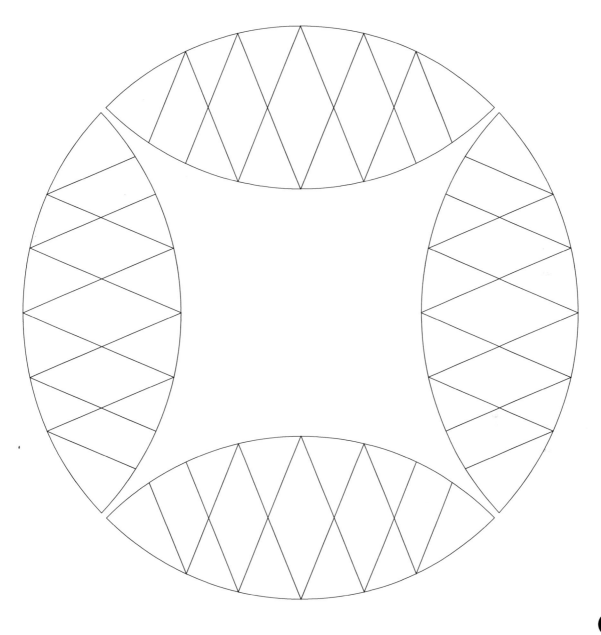

INTENTION: _____

_____

_____

_____

WEALTH

1. Where in my life do I act like this, but I'm not able to see it? Where do I express this quality without realizing it? Where do I feel like this?

_____

_____

_____

_____

_____

2. What is the positive aspect of this quality, emotion, or behavior? What could be its benefit?

_____

_____

_____

_____

_____

3. What is the negative aspect of this quality, emotion, or behavior? What drawbacks can it have?

_____

_____

_____

_____

_____

4. Where could I start expressing the positive aspect of this quality, emotion, or behavior in my life?

_____

_____

_____

_____

_____

INTENTION:

IRRESPONSIBILITY

1. Where in my life do I act like this, but I'm not able to see it? Where do I express this quality without realizing it? Where do I feel like this?

_____

_____

_____

_____

_____

2. What is the positive aspect of this quality, emotion, or behavior? What could be its benefit?

_____

_____

_____

_____

_____

3. What is the negative aspect of this quality, emotion, or behavior? What drawbacks can it have?

_____

_____

_____

_____

_____

4. Where could I start expressing the positive aspect of this quality, emotion, or behavior in my life?

_____

_____

_____

_____

_____

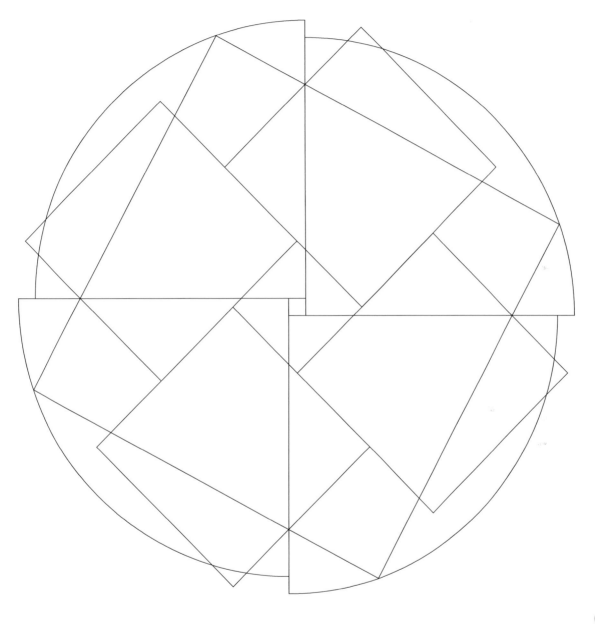

INTENTION:

RESPONSIBILITY

1. Where in my life do I act like this, but I'm not able to see it? Where do I express this quality without realizing it? Where do I feel like this?

_____

_____

_____

_____

_____

_____

2. What is the positive aspect of this quality, emotion, or behavior? What could be its benefit?

_____

_____

_____

_____

_____

3. What is the negative aspect of this quality, emotion, or behavior? What drawbacks can it have?

_____

_____

_____

_____

_____

4. Where could I start expressing the positive aspect of this quality, emotion, or behavior in my life?

_____

_____

_____

_____

_____

_____

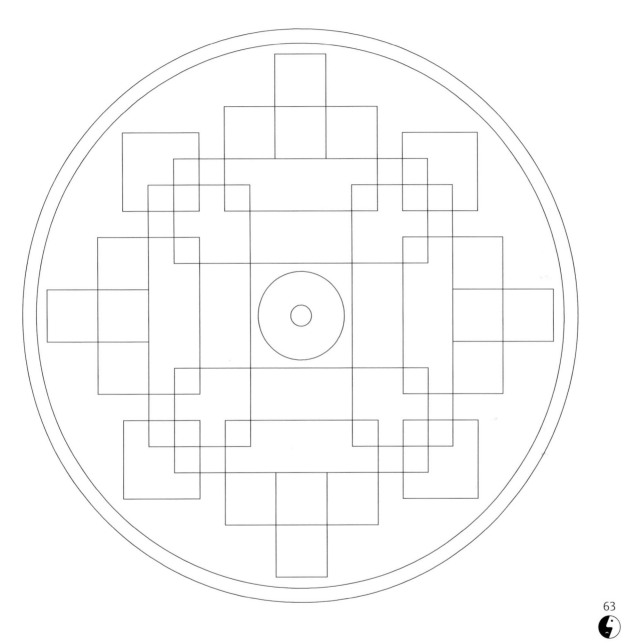

INTENTION:

INDECISIVENESS

1. Where in my life do I act like this, but I'm not able to see it? Where do I express this quality without realizing it? Where do I feel like this?

_____

_____

_____

_____

_____

_____

2. What is the positive aspect of this quality, emotion, or behavior? What could be its benefit?

_____

_____

_____

_____

_____

3. What is the negative aspect of this quality, emotion, or behavior? What drawbacks can it have?

_____

_____

_____

_____

4. Where could I start expressing the positive aspect of this quality, emotion, or behavior in my life?

_____

_____

_____

_____

_____

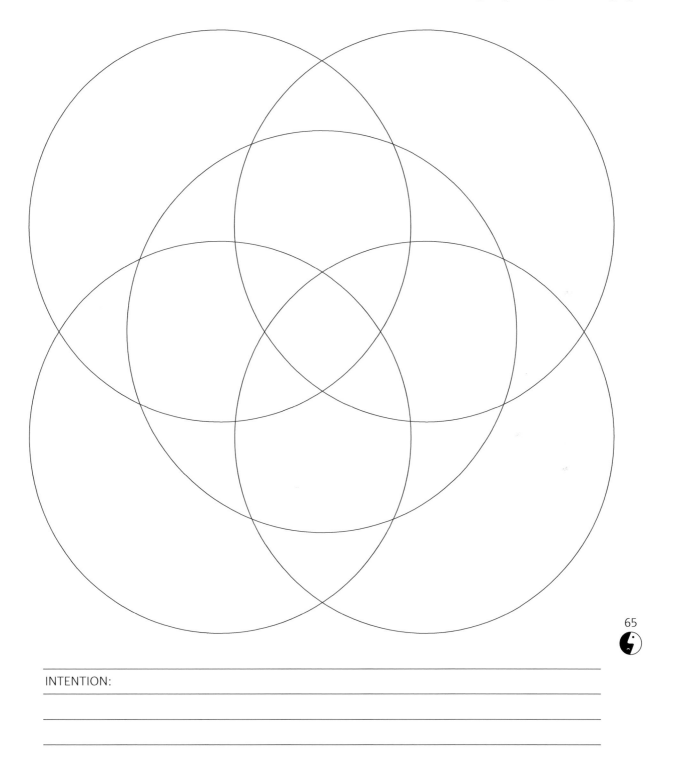

INTENTION: _____
_____
_____
_____

DECISIVENESS

1. Where in my life do I act like this, but I'm not able to see it? Where do I express this quality without realizing it? Where do I feel like this?

_____

_____

_____

_____

_____

_____

2. What is the positive aspect of this quality, emotion, or behavior? What could be its benefit?

_____

_____

_____

_____

_____

3. What is the negative aspect of this quality, emotion, or behavior? What drawbacks can it have?

_____

_____

_____

_____

_____

4. Where could I start expressing the positive aspect of this quality, emotion, or behavior in my life?

_____

_____

_____

_____

_____

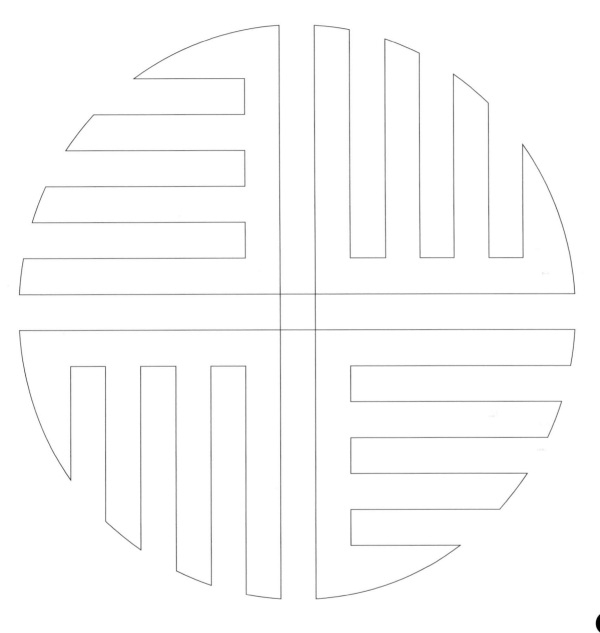

INTENTION:

FEAR

1. Where in my life do I act like this, but I'm not able to see it? Where do I express this quality without
   realizing it? Where do I feel like this?

_____

_____

_____

_____

_____

_____

2. What is the positive aspect of this quality, emotion, or behavior? What could be its benefit?

_____

_____

_____

_____

_____

3. What is the negative aspect of this quality, emotion, or behavior? What drawbacks can it have?

_____

_____

_____

_____

_____

4. Where could I start expressing the positive aspect of this quality, emotion, or behavior in my life?

_____

_____

_____

_____

_____

INTENTION:

COURAGE

1. Where in my life do I act like this, but I'm not able to see it? Where do I express this quality without realizing it? Where do I feel like this?

_____

_____

_____

_____

_____

_____

2. What is the positive aspect of this quality, emotion, or behavior? What could be its benefit?

_____

_____

_____

_____

_____

3. What is the negative aspect of this quality, emotion, or behavior? What drawbacks can it have?

_____

_____

_____

_____

_____

4. Where could I start expressing the positive aspect of this quality, emotion, or behavior in my life?

_____

_____

_____

_____

_____

INTENTION:

LONELINESS

1. Where in my life do I act like this, but I'm not able to see it? Where do I express this quality without realizing it? Where do I feel like this?

_____

_____

_____

_____

_____

_____

2. What is the positive aspect of this quality, emotion, or behavior? What could be its benefit?

_____

_____

_____

_____

_____

_____

3. What is the negative aspect of this quality, emotion, or behavior? What drawbacks can it have?

_____

_____

_____

_____

_____

_____

4. Where could I start expressing the positive aspect of this quality, emotion, or behavior in my life?

_____

_____

_____

_____

_____

_____

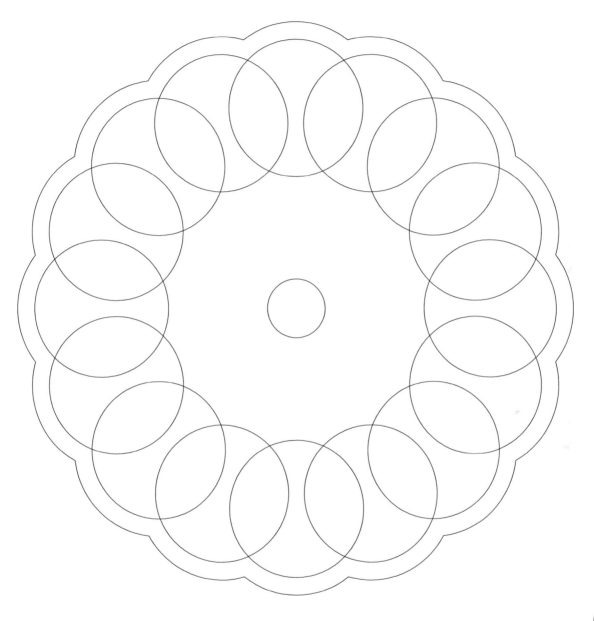

INTENTION:

RELATIONSHIP

1. Where in my life do I act like this, but I'm not able to see it? Where do I express this quality without realizing it? Where do I feel like this?

_____

_____

_____

_____

_____

2. What is the positive aspect of this quality, emotion, or behavior? What could be its benefit?

_____

_____

_____

_____

3. What is the negative aspect of this quality, emotion, or behavior? What drawbacks can it have?

_____

_____

_____

_____

4. Where could I start expressing the positive aspect of this quality, emotion, or behavior in my life?

_____

_____

_____

_____

INTENTION:

HATRED

1. Where in my life do I act like this, but I'm not able to see it? Where do I express this quality without realizing it? Where do I feel like this?

_____

_____

_____

_____

_____

2. What is the positive aspect of this quality, emotion, or behavior? What could be its benefit?

_____

_____

_____

_____

_____

3. What is the negative aspect of this quality, emotion, or behavior? What drawbacks can it have?

_____

_____

_____

_____

_____

4. Where could I start expressing the positive aspect of this quality, emotion, or behavior in my life?

_____

_____

_____

_____

_____

INTENTION:

LOVE

1. Where in my life do I act like this, but I'm not able to see it? Where do I express this quality without realizing it? Where do I feel like this?

_____

_____

_____

_____

_____

_____

2. What is the positive aspect of this quality, emotion, or behavior? What could be its benefit?

_____

_____

_____

_____

_____

3. What is the negative aspect of this quality, emotion, or behavior? What drawbacks can it have?

_____

_____

_____

_____

_____

4. Where could I start expressing the positive aspect of this quality, emotion, or behavior in my life?

_____

_____

_____

_____

_____

INTENTION:

INFERIORITY

1. Where in my life do I act like this, but I'm not able to see it? Where do I express this quality without realizing it? Where do I feel like this?

_____

_____

_____

_____

_____

_____

2. What is the positive aspect of this quality, emotion, or behavior? What could be its benefit?

_____

_____

_____

_____

_____

3. What is the negative aspect of this quality, emotion, or behavior? What drawbacks can it have?

_____

_____

_____

_____

_____

4. Where could I start expressing the positive aspect of this quality, emotion, or behavior in my life?

_____

_____

_____

_____

_____

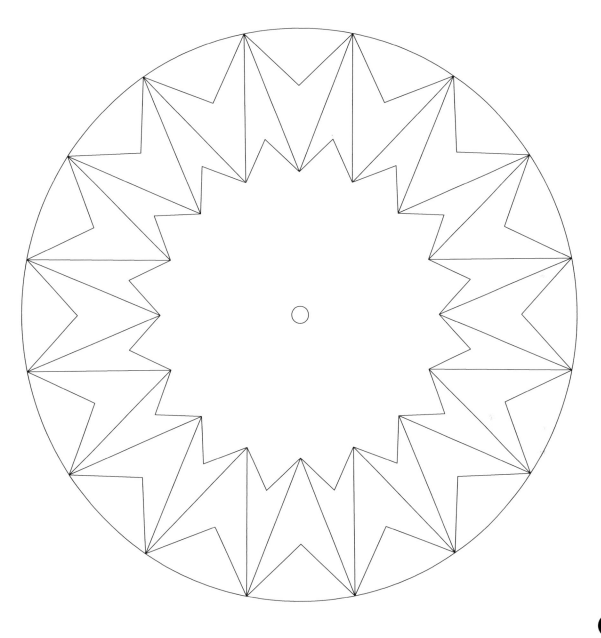

INTENTION:
_____
_____
_____
_____

SELF-CONFIDENCE

1. Where in my life do I act like this, but I'm not able to see it? Where do I express this quality without realizing it? Where do I feel like this?

_____

_____

_____

_____

_____

_____

_____

2. What is the positive aspect of this quality, emotion, or behavior? What could be its benefit?

_____

_____

_____

_____

_____

_____

3. What is the negative aspect of this quality, emotion, or behavior? What drawbacks can it have?

_____

_____

_____

_____

_____

_____

4. Where could I start expressing the positive aspect of this quality, emotion, or behavior in my life?

_____

_____

_____

_____

_____

_____

INTENTION:

INJUSTICE

1. Where in my life do I act like this, but I'm not able to see it? Where do I express this quality without realizing it? Where do I feel like this?

_____

_____

_____

_____

_____

_____

2. What is the positive aspect of this quality, emotion, or behavior? What could be its benefit?

_____

_____

_____

_____

_____

_____

3. What is the negative aspect of this quality, emotion, or behavior? What drawbacks can it have?

_____

_____

_____

_____

_____

4. Where could I start expressing the positive aspect of this quality, emotion, or behavior in my life?

_____

_____

_____

_____

_____

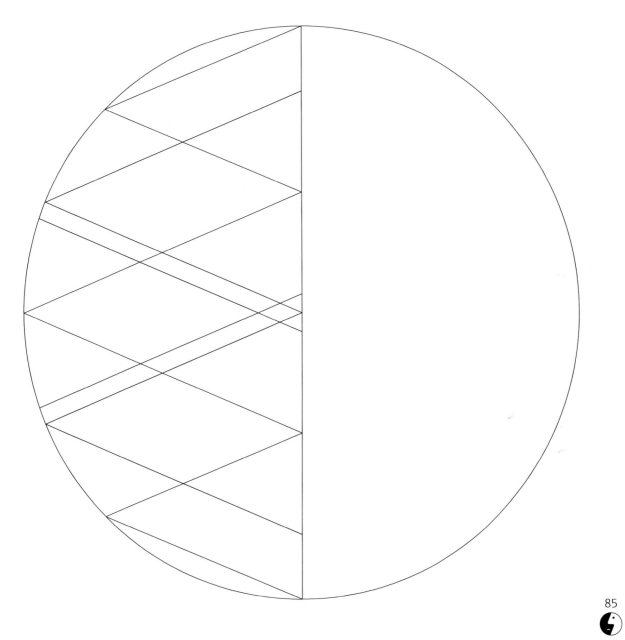

INTENTION:

JUSTICE

1. Where in my life do I act like this, but I'm not able to see it? Where do I express this quality without realizing it? Where do I feel like this?

_____
_____
_____
_____
_____
_____

2. What is the positive aspect of this quality, emotion, or behavior? What could be its benefit?

_____
_____
_____
_____
_____
_____

3. What is the negative aspect of this quality, emotion, or behavior? What drawbacks can it have?

_____
_____
_____
_____
_____
_____

4. Where could I start expressing the positive aspect of this quality, emotion, or behavior in my life?

_____
_____
_____
_____
_____

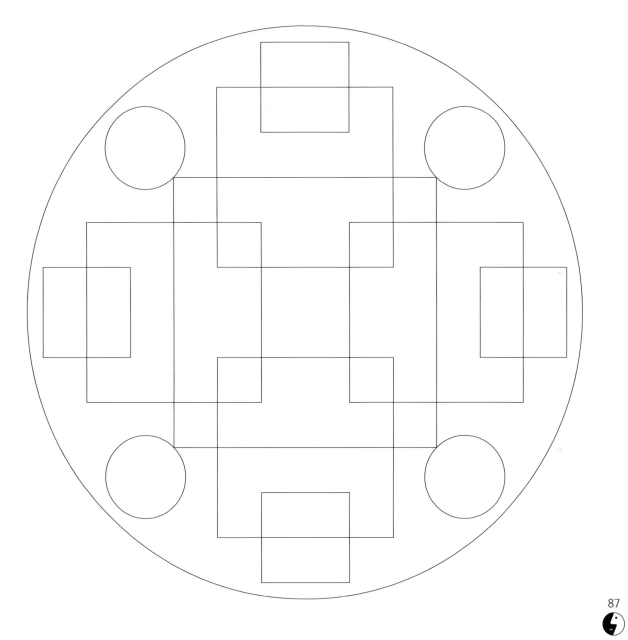

INTENTION:

INSECURITY

1. Where in my life do I act like this, but I'm not able to see it? Where do I express this quality without realizing it? Where do I feel like this?

_____

_____

_____

_____

_____

2. What is the positive aspect of this quality, emotion, or behavior? What could be its benefit?

_____

_____

_____

_____

3. What is the negative aspect of this quality, emotion, or behavior? What drawbacks can it have?

_____

_____

_____

_____

4. Where could I start expressing the positive aspect of this quality, emotion, or behavior in my life?

_____

_____

_____

_____

_____

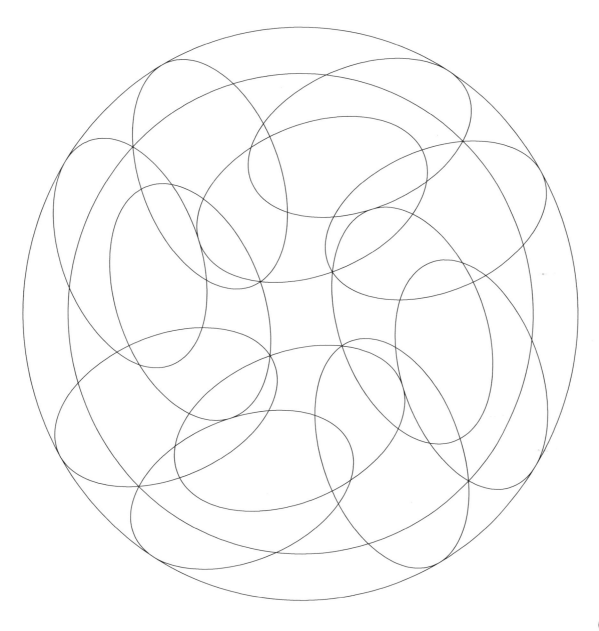

INTENTION:

SECURITY

1. Where in my life do I act like this, but I'm not able to see it? Where do I express this quality without realizing it? Where do I feel like this?

_____

_____

_____

_____

_____

_____

2. What is the positive aspect of this quality, emotion, or behavior? What could be its benefit?

_____

_____

_____

_____

_____

3. What is the negative aspect of this quality, emotion, or behavior? What drawbacks can it have?

_____

_____

_____

_____

_____

4. Where could I start expressing the positive aspect of this quality, emotion, or behavior in my life?

_____

_____

_____

_____

_____

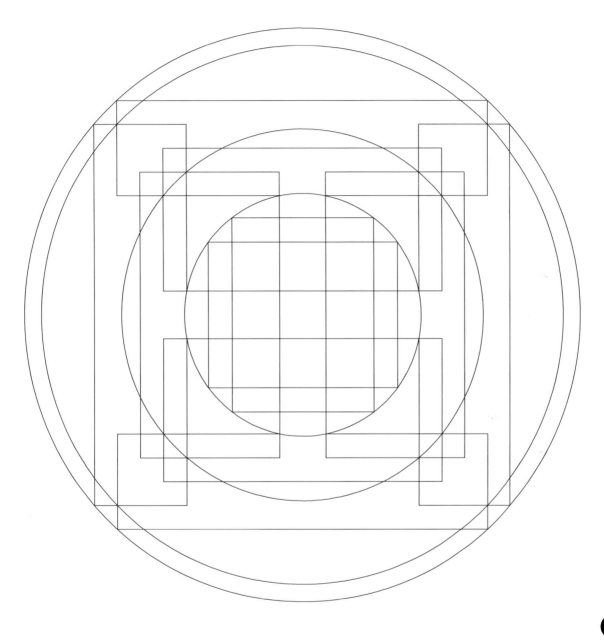

INTENTION:

UNGRATEFULNESS

1. Where in my life do I act like this, but I'm not able to see it? Where do I express this quality without realizing it? Where do I feel like this?

_____

_____

_____

_____

_____

_____

2. What is the positive aspect of this quality, emotion, or behavior? What could be its benefit?

_____

_____

_____

_____

_____

3. What is the negative aspect of this quality, emotion, or behavior? What drawbacks can it have?

_____

_____

_____

_____

_____

4. Where could I start expressing the positive aspect of this quality, emotion, or behavior in my life?

_____

_____

_____

_____

_____

INTENTION:

GRATEFULNESS

1. Where in my life do I act like this, but I'm not able to see it? Where do I express this quality without realizing it? Where do I feel like this?

_____

_____

_____

_____

_____

2. What is the positive aspect of this quality, emotion, or behavior? What could be its benefit?

_____

_____

_____

_____

_____

3. What is the negative aspect of this quality, emotion, or behavior? What drawbacks can it have?

_____

_____

_____

_____

_____

4. Where could I start expressing the positive aspect of this quality, emotion, or behavior in my life?

_____

_____

_____

_____

_____

INTENTION:

STRESS

1. Where in my life do I act like this, but I'm not able to see it? Where do I express this quality without realizing it? Where do I feel like this?

_____

_____

_____

_____

_____

_____

2. What is the positive aspect of this quality, emotion, or behavior? What could be its benefit?

_____

_____

_____

_____

_____

3. What is the negative aspect of this quality, emotion, or behavior? What drawbacks can it have?

_____

_____

_____

_____

_____

4. Where could I start expressing the positive aspect of this quality, emotion, or behavior in my life?

_____

_____

_____

_____

_____

INTENTION:

TRANQUILITY

1. Where in my life do I act like this, but I'm not able to see it? Where do I express this quality without realizing it? Where do I feel like this?

_____

_____

_____

_____

_____

2. What is the positive aspect of this quality, emotion, or behavior? What could be its benefit?

_____

_____

_____

_____

_____

3. What is the negative aspect of this quality, emotion, or behavior? What drawbacks can it have?

_____

_____

_____

_____

_____

4. Where could I start expressing the positive aspect of this quality, emotion, or behavior in my life?

_____

_____

_____

_____

_____

INTENTION:

OVERWEIGHT

1. Where in my life do I act like this, but I'm not able to see it? Where do I express this quality without realizing it? Where do I feel like this?

_____

_____

_____

_____

_____

_____

2. What is the positive aspect of this quality, emotion, or behavior? What could be its benefit?

_____

_____

_____

_____

_____

_____

3. What is the negative aspect of this quality, emotion, or behavior? What drawbacks can it have?

_____

_____

_____

_____

_____

_____

4. Where could I start expressing the positive aspect of this quality, emotion, or behavior in my life?

_____

_____

_____

_____

_____

INTENTION:

SLENDERNESS

1. Where in my life do I act like this, but I'm not able to see it? Where do I express this quality without realizing it? Where do I feel like this?

_____
_____
_____
_____
_____
_____

2. What is the positive aspect of this quality, emotion, or behavior? What could be its benefit?

_____
_____
_____
_____
_____
_____

3. What is the negative aspect of this quality, emotion, or behavior? What drawbacks can it have?

_____
_____
_____
_____
_____

4. Where could I start expressing the positive aspect of this quality, emotion, or behavior in my life?

_____
_____
_____
_____
_____
_____

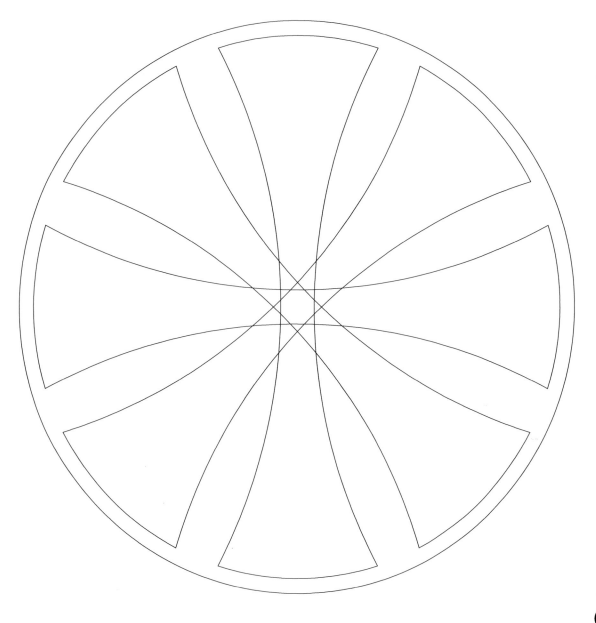

INTENTION:
_____

_____

_____

_____

SICKNESS

1. Where in my life do I act like this, but I'm not able to see it? Where do I express this quality without realizing it? Where do I feel like this?

_____

_____

_____

_____

_____

_____

2. What is the positive aspect of this quality, emotion, or behavior? What could be its benefit?

_____

_____

_____

_____

_____

_____

3. What is the negative aspect of this quality, emotion, or behavior? What drawbacks can it have?

_____

_____

_____

_____

_____

4. Where could I start expressing the positive aspect of this quality, emotion, or behavior in my life?

_____

_____

_____

_____

_____

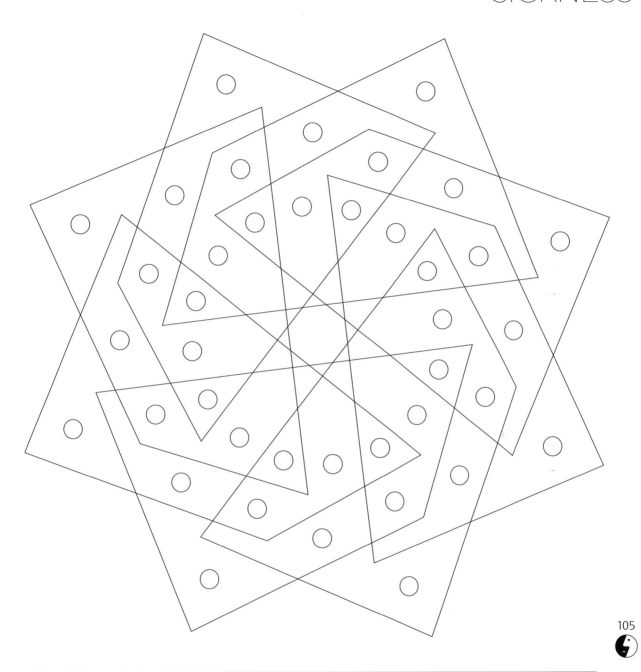

INTENTION:

HEALTH

1. Where in my life do I act like this, but I'm not able to see it? Where do I express this quality without realizing it? Where do I feel like this?

_____

_____

_____

_____

_____

_____

2. What is the positive aspect of this quality, emotion, or behavior? What could be its benefit?

_____

_____

_____

_____

_____

3. What is the negative aspect of this quality, emotion, or behavior? What drawbacks can it have?

_____

_____

_____

_____

_____

4. Where could I start expressing the positive aspect of this quality, emotion, or behavior in my life?

_____

_____

_____

_____

_____

INTENTION:

DEPENDENCE

1. Where in my life do I act like this, but I'm not able to see it? Where do I express this quality without realizing it? Where do I feel like this?

_____

_____

_____

_____

_____

_____

2. What is the positive aspect of this quality, emotion, or behavior? What could be its benefit?

_____

_____

_____

_____

_____

_____

3. What is the negative aspect of this quality, emotion, or behavior? What drawbacks can it have?

_____

_____

_____

_____

_____

_____

4. Where could I start expressing the positive aspect of this quality, emotion, or behavior in my life?

_____

_____

_____

_____

_____

_____

INTENTION: _____

_____

_____

_____

INDEPENDENCE

1. Where in my life do I act like this, but I'm not able to see it? Where do I express this quality without realizing it? Where do I feel like this?

_____

_____

_____

_____

_____

_____

2. What is the positive aspect of this quality, emotion, or behavior? What could be its benefit?

_____

_____

_____

_____

_____

_____

3. What is the negative aspect of this quality, emotion, or behavior? What drawbacks can it have?

_____

_____

_____

_____

_____

_____

4. Where could I start expressing the positive aspect of this quality, emotion, or behavior in my life?

_____

_____

_____

_____

_____

_____

INTENTION:

CONTROL

1. Where in my life do I act like this, but I'm not able to see it? Where do I express this quality without realizing it? Where do I feel like this?

_____

_____

_____

_____

_____

_____

2. What is the positive aspect of this quality, emotion, or behavior? What could be its benefit?

_____

_____

_____

_____

_____

3. What is the negative aspect of this quality, emotion, or behavior? What drawbacks can it have?

_____

_____

_____

_____

_____

4. Where could I start expressing the positive aspect of this quality, emotion, or behavior in my life?

_____

_____

_____

_____

_____

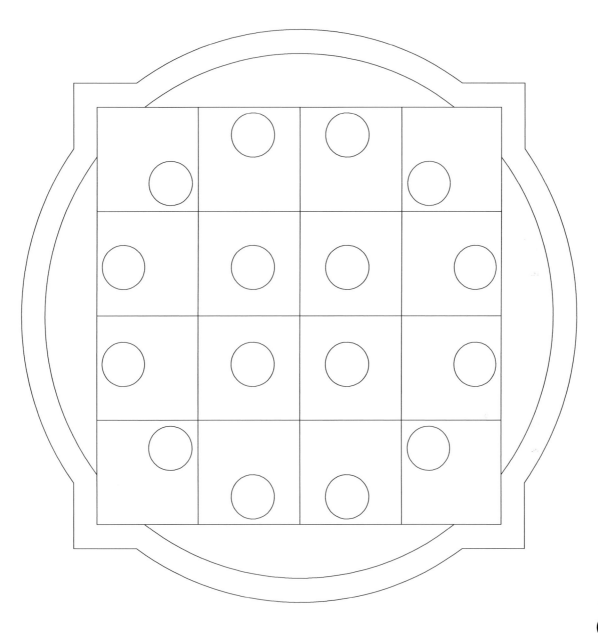

INTENTION:

FREEDOM

1. Where in my life do I act like this, but I'm not able to see it? Where do I express this quality without realizing it? Where do I feel like this?

_____

_____

_____

_____

_____

_____

2. What is the positive aspect of this quality, emotion, or behavior? What could be its benefit?

_____

_____

_____

_____

_____

_____

3. What is the negative aspect of this quality, emotion, or behavior? What drawbacks can it have?

_____

_____

_____

_____

_____

_____

4. Where could I start expressing the positive aspect of this quality, emotion, or behavior in my life?

_____

_____

_____

_____

_____

_____

INTENTION:

LYING

1. Where in my life do I act like this, but I'm not able to see it? Where do I express this quality without
   realizing it? Where do I feel like this?

_____

_____

_____

_____

_____

_____

2. What is the positive aspect of this quality, emotion, or behavior? What could be its benefit?

_____

_____

_____

_____

_____

3. What is the negative aspect of this quality, emotion, or behavior? What drawbacks can it have?

_____

_____

_____

_____

_____

4. Where could I start expressing the positive aspect of this quality, emotion, or behavior in my life?

_____

_____

_____

_____

_____

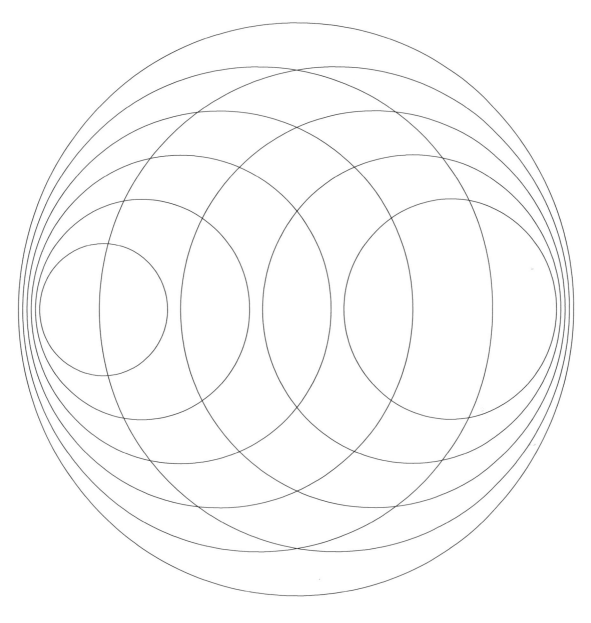

INTENTION:

TRUTHFULNESS

1. Where in my life do I act like this, but I'm not able to see it? Where do I express this quality without realizing it? Where do I feel like this?

_____

_____

_____

_____

_____

_____

2. What is the positive aspect of this quality, emotion, or behavior? What could be its benefit?

_____

_____

_____

_____

_____

_____

3. What is the negative aspect of this quality, emotion, or behavior? What drawbacks can it have?

_____

_____

_____

_____

_____

_____

4. Where could I start expressing the positive aspect of this quality, emotion, or behavior in my life?

_____

_____

_____

_____

_____

_____

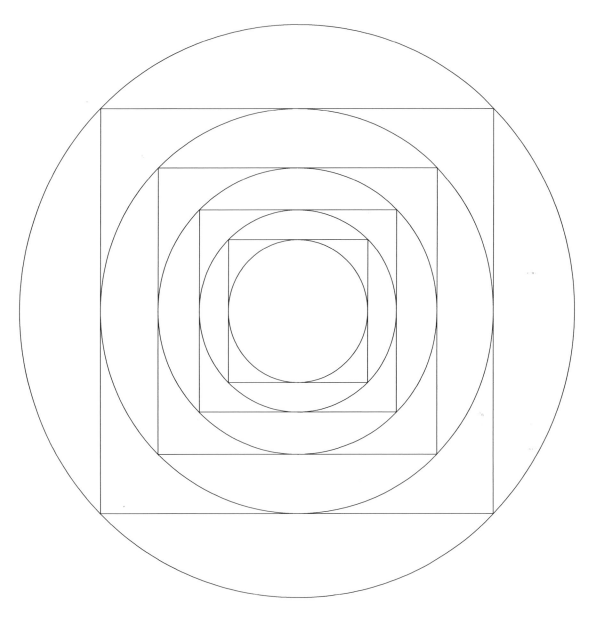

INTENTION:

DESPAIR

1. Where in my life do I act like this, but I'm not able to see it? Where do I express this quality without realizing it? Where do I feel like this?

_____

_____

_____

_____

_____

_____

2. What is the positive aspect of this quality, emotion, or behavior? What could be its benefit?

_____

_____

_____

_____

_____

_____

3. What is the negative aspect of this quality, emotion, or behavior? What drawbacks can it have?

_____

_____

_____

_____

_____

_____

4. Where could I start expressing the positive aspect of this quality, emotion, or behavior in my life?

_____

_____

_____

_____

_____

_____

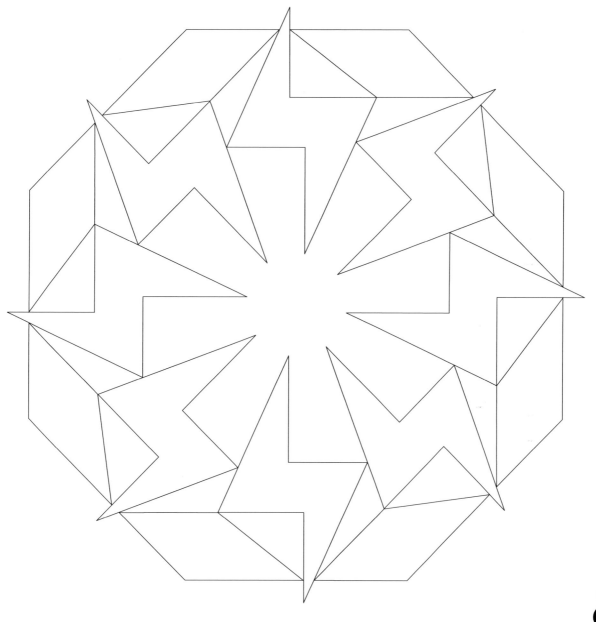

INTENTION:

HOPE

1. Where in my life do I act like this, but I'm not able to see it? Where do I express this quality without realizing it? Where do I feel like this?

_____

_____

_____

_____

_____

2. What is the positive aspect of this quality, emotion, or behavior? What could be its benefit?

_____

_____

_____

_____

_____

3. What is the negative aspect of this quality, emotion, or behavior? What drawbacks can it have?

_____

_____

_____

_____

_____

4. Where could I start expressing the positive aspect of this quality, emotion, or behavior in my life?

_____

_____

_____

_____

_____

_____

INTENTION:

SELF-INDULGENCE

1. Where in my life do I act like this, but I'm not able to see it? Where do I express this quality without realizing it? Where do I feel like this?

_____

_____

_____

_____

_____

_____

2. What is the positive aspect of this quality, emotion, or behavior? What could be its benefit?

_____

_____

_____

_____

_____

_____

3. What is the negative aspect of this quality, emotion, or behavior? What drawbacks can it have?

_____

_____

_____

_____

_____

_____

4. Where could I start expressing the positive aspect of this quality, emotion, or behavior in my life?

_____

_____

_____

_____

_____

_____

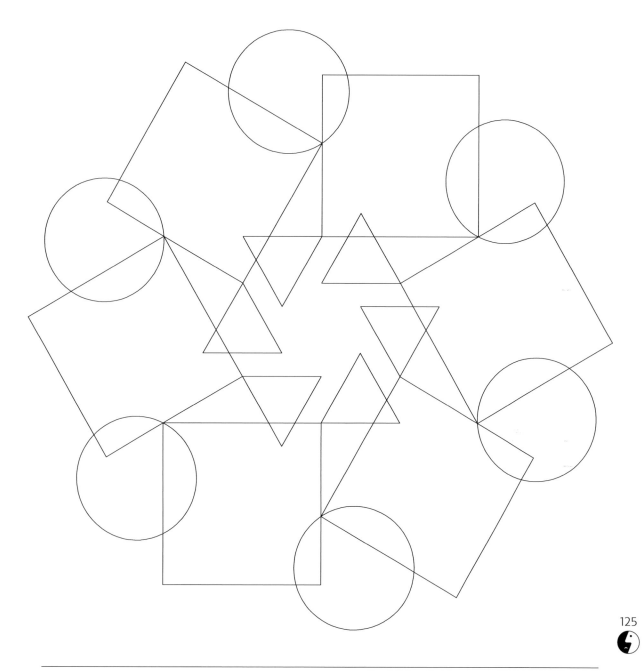

INTENTION:

SELF-DISCIPLINE

1. Where in my life do I act like this, but I'm not able to see it? Where do I express this quality without realizing it? Where do I feel like this?

_____
_____
_____
_____
_____
_____

2. What is the positive aspect of this quality, emotion, or behavior? What could be its benefit?

_____
_____
_____
_____
_____
_____

3. What is the negative aspect of this quality, emotion, or behavior? What drawbacks can it have?

_____
_____
_____
_____
_____

4. Where could I start expressing the positive aspect of this quality, emotion, or behavior in my life?

_____
_____
_____
_____
_____

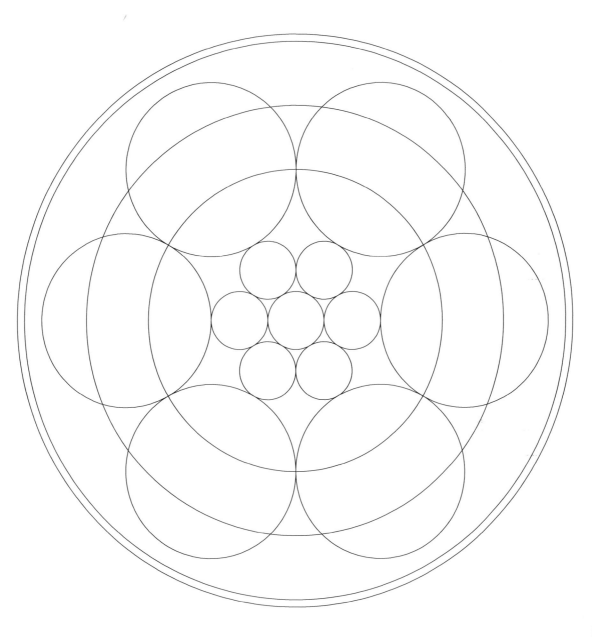

INTENTION:

DISHONESTY

1. Where in my life do I act like this, but I'm not able to see it? Where do I express this quality without realizing it? Where do I feel like this?

_____
_____
_____
_____
_____
_____

2. What is the positive aspect of this quality, emotion, or behavior? What could be its benefit?

_____
_____
_____
_____
_____
_____

3. What is the negative aspect of this quality, emotion, or behavior? What drawbacks can it have?

_____
_____
_____
_____
_____
_____

4. Where could I start expressing the positive aspect of this quality, emotion, or behavior in my life?

_____
_____
_____
_____
_____
_____

INTENTION: _____

_____

_____

_____

HONESTY

1. Where in my life do I act like this, but I'm not able to see it? Where do I express this quality without realizing it? Where do I feel like this?

_____

_____

_____

_____

_____

2. What is the positive aspect of this quality, emotion, or behavior? What could be its benefit?

_____

_____

_____

_____

_____

3. What is the negative aspect of this quality, emotion, or behavior? What drawbacks can it have?

_____

_____

_____

_____

_____

4. Where could I start expressing the positive aspect of this quality, emotion, or behavior in my life?

_____

_____

_____

_____

_____

_____

INTENTION: _____

_____

_____

_____

INCOMPETENCE

1. Where in my life do I act like this, but I'm not able to see it? Where do I express this quality without realizing it? Where do I feel like this?

_____

_____

_____

_____

_____

2. What is the positive aspect of this quality, emotion, or behavior? What could be its benefit?

_____

_____

_____

_____

_____

3. What is the negative aspect of this quality, emotion, or behavior? What drawbacks can it have?

_____

_____

_____

_____

_____

4. Where could I start expressing the positive aspect of this quality, emotion, or behavior in my life?

_____

_____

_____

_____

_____

INTENTION:

COMPETENCE

1. Where in my life do I act like this, but I'm not able to see it? Where do I express this quality without realizing it? Where do I feel like this?

_____

_____

_____

_____

_____

_____

2. What is the positive aspect of this quality, emotion, or behavior? What could be its benefit?

_____

_____

_____

_____

_____

_____

3. What is the negative aspect of this quality, emotion, or behavior? What drawbacks can it have?

_____

_____

_____

_____

_____

4. Where could I start expressing the positive aspect of this quality, emotion, or behavior in my life?

_____

_____

_____

_____

_____

_____

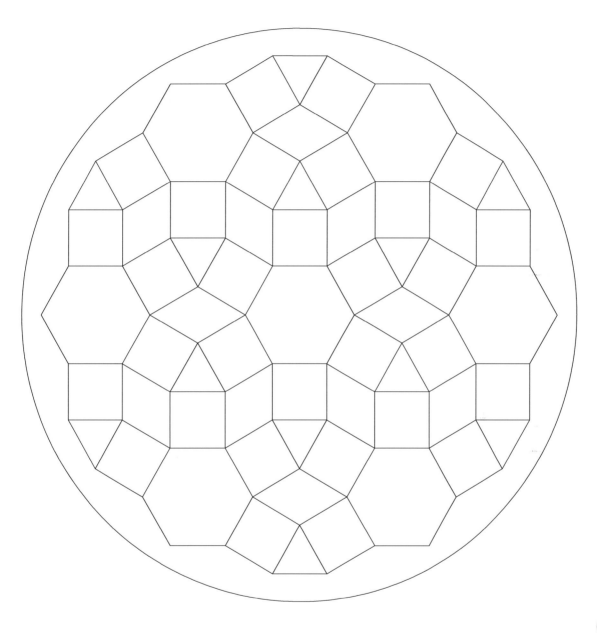

INTENTION:

INADAPTABILITY

1. Where in my life do I act like this, but I'm not able to see it? Where do I express this quality without realizing it? Where do I feel like this?

_____

_____

_____

_____

_____

_____

2. What is the positive aspect of this quality, emotion, or behavior? What could be its benefit?

_____

_____

_____

_____

_____

3. What is the negative aspect of this quality, emotion, or behavior? What drawbacks can it have?

_____

_____

_____

_____

4. Where could I start expressing the positive aspect of this quality, emotion, or behavior in my life?

_____

_____

_____

_____

_____

INTENTION:

ADAPTABILITY

1. Where in my life do I act like this, but I'm not able to see it? Where do I express this quality without realizing it? Where do I feel like this?

_____

_____

_____

_____

_____

_____

2. What is the positive aspect of this quality, emotion, or behavior? What could be its benefit?

_____

_____

_____

_____

_____

_____

3. What is the negative aspect of this quality, emotion, or behavior? What drawbacks can it have?

_____

_____

_____

_____

_____

_____

4. Where could I start expressing the positive aspect of this quality, emotion, or behavior in my life?

_____

_____

_____

_____

_____

_____

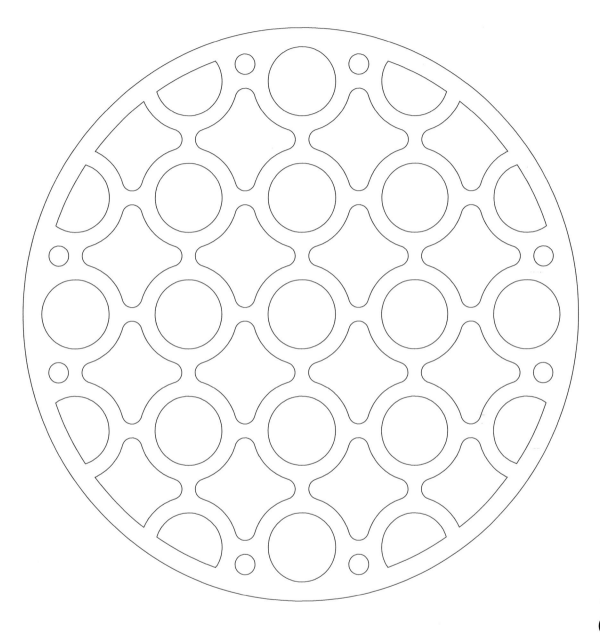

INTENTION:
_____
_____
_____
_____

LAZINESS

1. Where in my life do I act like this, but I'm not able to see it? Where do I express this quality without realizing it? Where do I feel like this?

_____

_____

_____

_____

_____

2. What is the positive aspect of this quality, emotion, or behavior? What could be its benefit?

_____

_____

_____

_____

_____

3. What is the negative aspect of this quality, emotion, or behavior? What drawbacks can it have?

_____

_____

_____

_____

_____

4. Where could I start expressing the positive aspect of this quality, emotion, or behavior in my life?

_____

_____

_____

_____

_____

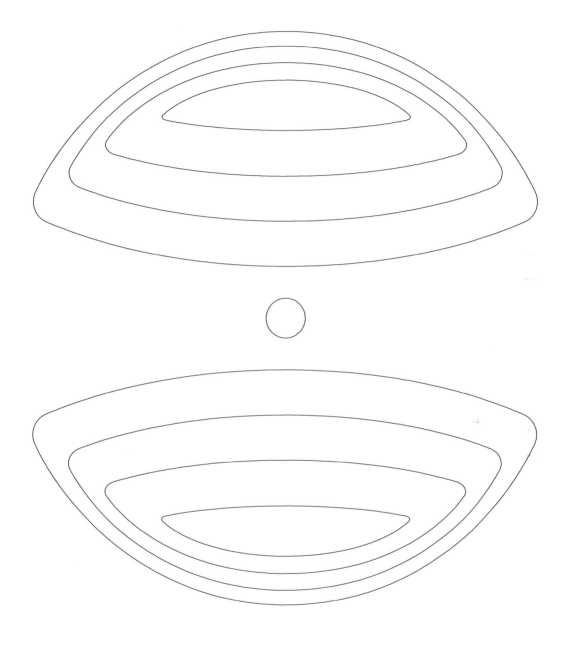

INTENTION:

DILIGENCE

1. Where in my life do I act like this, but I'm not able to see it? Where do I express this quality without realizing it? Where do I feel like this?

_____

_____

_____

_____

_____

_____

2. What is the positive aspect of this quality, emotion, or behavior? What could be its benefit?

_____

_____

_____

_____

_____

_____

3. What is the negative aspect of this quality, emotion, or behavior? What drawbacks can it have?

_____

_____

_____

_____

_____

4. Where could I start expressing the positive aspect of this quality, emotion, or behavior in my life?

_____

_____

_____

_____

_____

_____

INTENTION:

REJECTION

1. Where in my life do I act like this, but I'm not able to see it? Where do I express this quality without realizing it? Where do I feel like this?

_____

_____

_____

_____

_____

_____

2. What is the positive aspect of this quality, emotion, or behavior? What could be its benefit?

_____

_____

_____

_____

_____

_____

3. What is the negative aspect of this quality, emotion, or behavior? What drawbacks can it have?

_____

_____

_____

_____

_____

4. Where could I start expressing the positive aspect of this quality, emotion, or behavior in my life?

_____

_____

_____

_____

_____

_____

INTENTION:

ACCEPTANCE

1. Where in my life do I act like this, but I'm not able to see it? Where do I express this quality without realizing it? Where do I feel like this?

_____

_____

_____

_____

_____

_____

2. What is the positive aspect of this quality, emotion, or behavior? What could be its benefit?

_____

_____

_____

_____

_____

_____

3. What is the negative aspect of this quality, emotion, or behavior? What drawbacks can it have?

_____

_____

_____

_____

_____

_____

4. Where could I start expressing the positive aspect of this quality, emotion, or behavior in my life?

_____

_____

_____

_____

_____

_____

INTENTION:

PASSIVITY

1. Where in my life do I act like this, but I'm not able to see it? Where do I express this quality without realizing it? Where do I feel like this?

_____
_____
_____
_____
_____
_____

2. What is the positive aspect of this quality, emotion, or behavior? What could be its benefit?

_____
_____
_____
_____
_____
_____

3. What is the negative aspect of this quality, emotion, or behavior? What drawbacks can it have?

_____
_____
_____
_____
_____
_____

4. Where could I start expressing the positive aspect of this quality, emotion, or behavior in my life?

_____
_____
_____
_____
_____

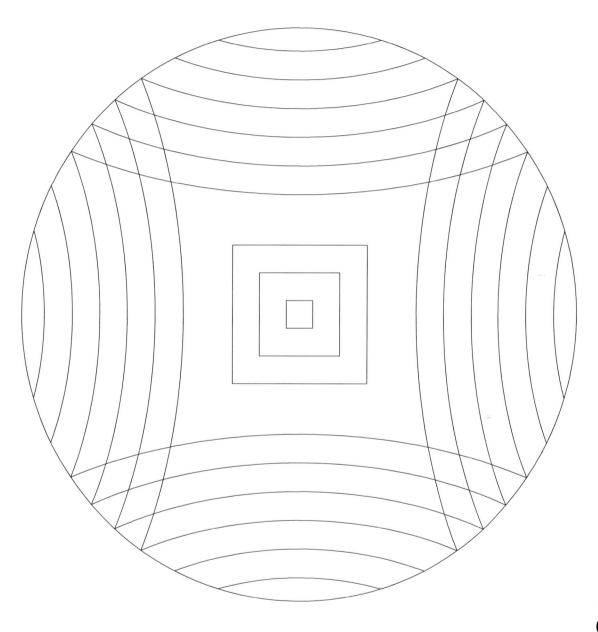

INTENTION:

ACTIVITY

1. Where in my life do I act like this, but I'm not able to see it? Where do I express this quality without realizing it? Where do I feel like this?

_____

_____

_____

_____

_____

2. What is the positive aspect of this quality, emotion, or behavior? What could be its benefit?

_____

_____

_____

_____

_____

3. What is the negative aspect of this quality, emotion, or behavior? What drawbacks can it have?

_____

_____

_____

_____

_____

4. Where could I start expressing the positive aspect of this quality, emotion, or behavior in my life?

_____

_____

_____

_____

_____

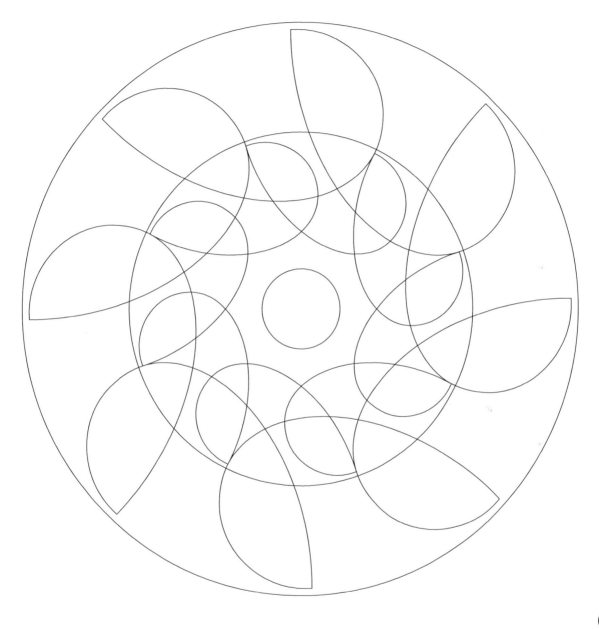

INTENTION: _____

_____

_____

_____

AFFECTATION

1. Where in my life do I act like this, but I'm not able to see it? Where do I express this quality without realizing it? Where do I feel like this?

_____

_____

_____

_____

_____

_____

2. What is the positive aspect of this quality, emotion, or behavior? What could be its benefit?

_____

_____

_____

_____

_____

_____

3. What is the negative aspect of this quality, emotion, or behavior? What drawbacks can it have?

_____

_____

_____

_____

_____

_____

4. Where could I start expressing the positive aspect of this quality, emotion, or behavior in my life?

_____

_____

_____

_____

_____

_____

153

INTENTION:

SPONTANEITY

1. Where in my life do I act like this, but I'm not able to see it? Where do I express this quality without realizing it? Where do I feel like this?

_____

_____

_____

_____

_____

2. What is the positive aspect of this quality, emotion, or behavior? What could be its benefit?

_____

_____

_____

_____

_____

3. What is the negative aspect of this quality, emotion, or behavior? What drawbacks can it have?

_____

_____

_____

_____

_____

4. Where could I start expressing the positive aspect of this quality, emotion, or behavior in my life?

_____

_____

_____

_____

_____

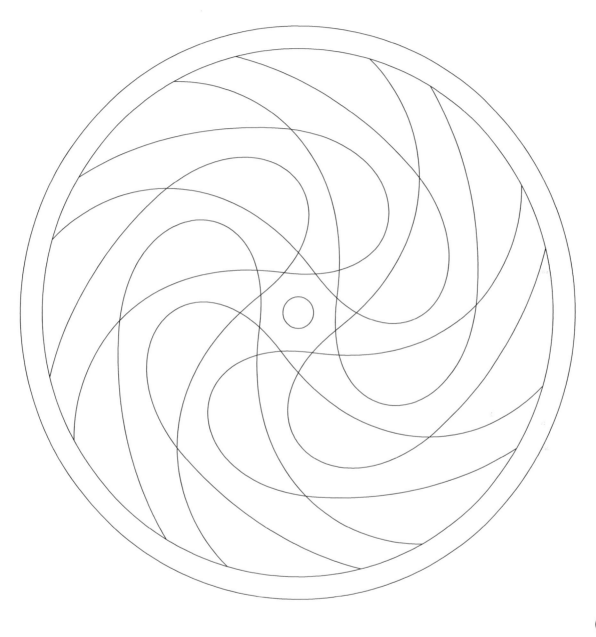

INTENTION:

WRONG DECISION

1. Where in my life do I act like this, but I'm not able to see it? Where do I express this quality without realizing it? Where do I feel like this?

_____

_____

_____

_____

_____

_____

2. What is the positive aspect of this quality, emotion, or behavior? What could be its benefit?

_____

_____

_____

_____

_____

_____

3. What is the negative aspect of this quality, emotion, or behavior? What drawbacks can it have?

_____

_____

_____

_____

_____

_____

4. Where could I start expressing the positive aspect of this quality, emotion, or behavior in my life?

_____

_____

_____

_____

_____

_____

INTENTION: _____

_____

_____

_____

RIGHT DECISION

1. Where in my life do I act like this, but I'm not able to see it? Where do I express this quality without realizing it? Where do I feel like this?

_____

_____

_____

_____

_____

_____

2. What is the positive aspect of this quality, emotion, or behavior? What could be its benefit?

_____

_____

_____

_____

_____

3. What is the negative aspect of this quality, emotion, or behavior? What drawbacks can it have?

_____

_____

_____

_____

_____

4. Where could I start expressing the positive aspect of this quality, emotion, or behavior in my life?

_____

_____

_____

_____

_____

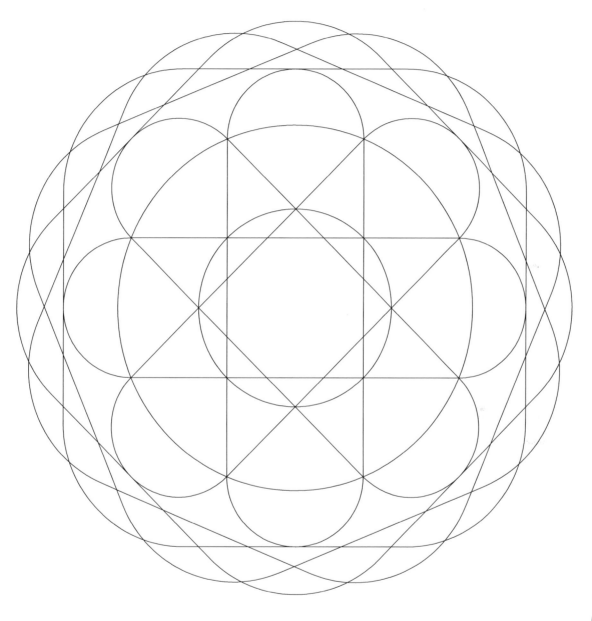

INTENTION:

LOSS

1. Where in my life do I act like this, but I'm not able to see it? Where do I express this quality without realizing it? Where do I feel like this?

_____

_____

_____

_____

_____

_____

2. What is the positive aspect of this quality, emotion, or behavior? What could be its benefit?

_____

_____

_____

_____

_____

_____

3. What is the negative aspect of this quality, emotion, or behavior? What drawbacks can it have?

_____

_____

_____

_____

_____

_____

4. Where could I start expressing the positive aspect of this quality, emotion, or behavior in my life?

_____

_____

_____

_____

_____

_____

INTENTION:
_____

_____

_____

_____

GAIN

1. Where in my life do I act like this, but I'm not able to see it? Where do I express this quality without realizing it? Where do I feel like this?

_____

_____

_____

_____

_____

_____

2. What is the positive aspect of this quality, emotion, or behavior? What could be its benefit?

_____

_____

_____

_____

_____

3. What is the negative aspect of this quality, emotion, or behavior? What drawbacks can it have?

_____

_____

_____

_____

_____

4. Where could I start expressing the positive aspect of this quality, emotion, or behavior in my life?

_____

_____

_____

_____

_____

INTENTION:

DISSATISFACTION

1. Where in my life do I act like this, but I'm not able to see it? Where do I express this quality without realizing it? Where do I feel like this?

_____

_____

_____

_____

_____

2. What is the positive aspect of this quality, emotion, or behavior? What could be its benefit?

_____

_____

_____

_____

_____

3. What is the negative aspect of this quality, emotion, or behavior? What drawbacks can it have?

_____

_____

_____

_____

_____

4. Where could I start expressing the positive aspect of this quality, emotion, or behavior in my life?

_____

_____

_____

_____

_____

INTENTION:

SATISFACTION

1. Where in my life do I act like this, but I'm not able to see it? Where do I express this quality without realizing it? Where do I feel like this?

_____

_____

_____

_____

_____

2. What is the positive aspect of this quality, emotion, or behavior? What could be its benefit?

_____

_____

_____

_____

_____

3. What is the negative aspect of this quality, emotion, or behavior? What drawbacks can it have?

_____

_____

_____

_____

_____

4. Where could I start expressing the positive aspect of this quality, emotion, or behavior in my life?

_____

_____

_____

_____

_____

INTENTION: _____

_____

_____

_____

CRISIS

1. Where in my life do I act like this, but I'm not able to see it? Where do I express this quality without realizing it? Where do I feel like this?

_____

_____

_____

_____

_____

_____

2. What is the positive aspect of this quality, emotion, or behavior? What could be its benefit?

_____

_____

_____

_____

_____

_____

3. What is the negative aspect of this quality, emotion, or behavior? What drawbacks can it have?

_____

_____

_____

_____

_____

4. Where could I start expressing the positive aspect of this quality, emotion, or behavior in my life?

_____

_____

_____

_____

_____

_____

INTENTION: _____

SOLUTION

1. Where in my life do I act like this, but I'm not able to see it? Where do I express this quality without realizing it? Where do I feel like this?

_____

_____

_____

_____

_____

2. What is the positive aspect of this quality, emotion, or behavior? What could be its benefit?

_____

_____

_____

_____

_____

3. What is the negative aspect of this quality, emotion, or behavior? What drawbacks can it have?

_____

_____

_____

_____

_____

4. Where could I start expressing the positive aspect of this quality, emotion, or behavior in my life?

_____

_____

_____

_____

_____

INTENTION:

INJURY

1. Where in my life do I act like this, but I'm not able to see it? Where do I express this quality without realizing it? Where do I feel like this?

_____

_____

_____

_____

_____

_____

2. What is the positive aspect of this quality, emotion, or behavior? What could be its benefit?

_____

_____

_____

_____

_____

_____

3. What is the negative aspect of this quality, emotion, or behavior? What drawbacks can it have?

_____

_____

_____

_____

_____

_____

4. Where could I start expressing the positive aspect of this quality, emotion, or behavior in my life?

_____

_____

_____

_____

_____

INTENTION:

HEALING

1. Where in my life do I act like this, but I'm not able to see it? Where do I express this quality without realizing it? Where do I feel like this?

_____

_____

_____

_____

_____

_____

2. What is the positive aspect of this quality, emotion, or behavior? What could be its benefit?

_____

_____

_____

_____

_____

_____

3. What is the negative aspect of this quality, emotion, or behavior? What drawbacks can it have?

_____

_____

_____

_____

_____

_____

4. Where could I start expressing the positive aspect of this quality, emotion, or behavior in my life?

_____

_____

_____

_____

_____

_____

INTENTION:

ENVY

1. Where in my life do I act like this, but I'm not able to see it? Where do I express this quality without realizing it? Where do I feel like this?

_____

_____

_____

_____

_____

2. What is the positive aspect of this quality, emotion, or behavior? What could be its benefit?

_____

_____

_____

_____

_____

3. What is the negative aspect of this quality, emotion, or behavior? What drawbacks can it have?

_____

_____

_____

_____

_____

4. Where could I start expressing the positive aspect of this quality, emotion, or behavior in my life?

_____

_____

_____

_____

_____

INTENTION:

GENEROSITY

1. Where in my life do I act like this, but I'm not able to see it? Where do I express this quality without realizing it? Where do I feel like this?

_____
_____
_____
_____
_____
_____

2. What is the positive aspect of this quality, emotion, or behavior? What could be its benefit?

_____
_____
_____
_____
_____
_____

3. What is the negative aspect of this quality, emotion, or behavior? What drawbacks can it have?

_____
_____
_____
_____
_____

4. Where could I start expressing the positive aspect of this quality, emotion, or behavior in my life?

_____
_____
_____
_____
_____
_____

INTENTION:

HOLDING BACK

1. Where in my life do I act like this, but I'm not able to see it? Where do I express this quality without realizing it? Where do I feel like this?

_____

_____

_____

_____

_____

_____

2. What is the positive aspect of this quality, emotion, or behavior? What could be its benefit?

_____

_____

_____

_____

_____

_____

3. What is the negative aspect of this quality, emotion, or behavior? What drawbacks can it have?

_____

_____

_____

_____

_____

_____

4. Where could I start expressing the positive aspect of this quality, emotion, or behavior in my life?

_____

_____

_____

_____

_____

_____

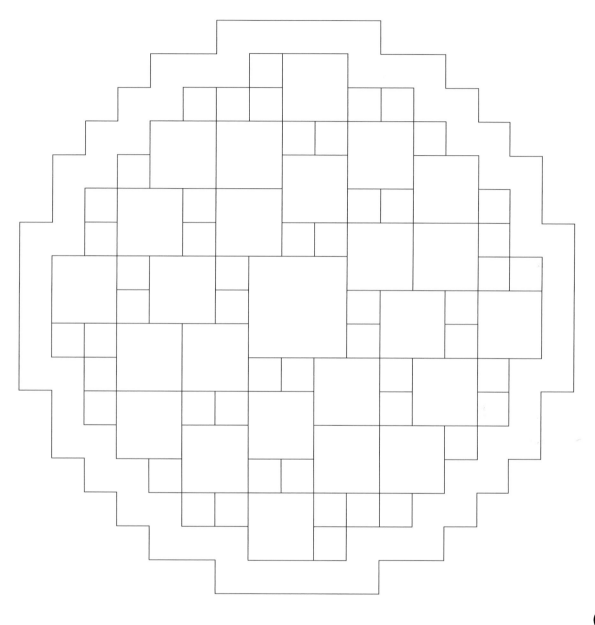

INTENTION:

LETTING GO

1. Where in my life do I act like this, but I'm not able to see it? Where do I express this quality without realizing it? Where do I feel like this?

_____

_____

_____

_____

_____

_____

2. What is the positive aspect of this quality, emotion, or behavior? What could be its benefit?

_____

_____

_____

_____

_____

_____

3. What is the negative aspect of this quality, emotion, or behavior? What drawbacks can it have?

_____

_____

_____

_____

_____

4. Where could I start expressing the positive aspect of this quality, emotion, or behavior in my life?

_____

_____

_____

_____

_____

INTENTION:

STAGNATION

1. Where in my life do I act like this, but I'm not able to see it? Where do I express this quality without realizing it? Where do I feel like this?

_____

_____

_____

_____

_____

_____

2. What is the positive aspect of this quality, emotion, or behavior? What could be its benefit?

_____

_____

_____

_____

_____

_____

3. What is the negative aspect of this quality, emotion, or behavior? What drawbacks can it have?

_____

_____

_____

_____

_____

4. Where could I start expressing the positive aspect of this quality, emotion, or behavior in my life?

_____

_____

_____

_____

_____

_____

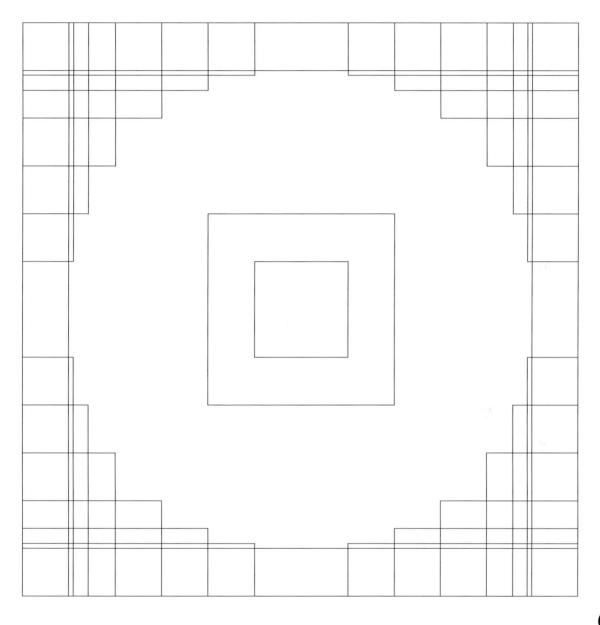

INTENTION:

GROWTH

1. Where in my life do I act like this, but I'm not able to see it? Where do I express this quality without realizing it? Where do I feel like this?

_____

_____

_____

_____

_____

_____

2. What is the positive aspect of this quality, emotion, or behavior? What could be its benefit?

_____

_____

_____

_____

_____

3. What is the negative aspect of this quality, emotion, or behavior? What drawbacks can it have?

_____

_____

_____

_____

_____

4. Where could I start expressing the positive aspect of this quality, emotion, or behavior in my life?

_____

_____

_____

_____

_____

INTENTION:

CARELESSNESS

1. Where in my life do I act like this, but I'm not able to see it? Where do I express this quality without realizing it? Where do I feel like this?

_____

_____

_____

_____

_____

2. What is the positive aspect of this quality, emotion, or behavior? What could be its benefit?

_____

_____

_____

_____

_____

3. What is the negative aspect of this quality, emotion, or behavior? What drawbacks can it have?

_____

_____

_____

_____

_____

4. Where could I start expressing the positive aspect of this quality, emotion, or behavior in my life?

_____

_____

_____

_____

_____

INTENTION:

THOUGHTFULNESS

1. Where in my life do I act like this, but I'm not able to see it? Where do I express this quality without realizing it? Where do I feel like this?

_____

_____

_____

_____

_____

_____

2. What is the positive aspect of this quality, emotion, or behavior? What could be its benefit?

_____

_____

_____

_____

_____

_____

3. What is the negative aspect of this quality, emotion, or behavior? What drawbacks can it have?

_____

_____

_____

_____

_____

4. Where could I start expressing the positive aspect of this quality, emotion, or behavior in my life?

_____

_____

_____

_____

_____

_____

INTENTION:

CRUELTY

1. Where in my life do I act like this, but I'm not able to see it? Where do I express this quality without realizing it? Where do I feel like this?

_____

_____

_____

_____

_____

_____

2. What is the positive aspect of this quality, emotion, or behavior? What could be its benefit?

_____

_____

_____

_____

_____

3. What is the negative aspect of this quality, emotion, or behavior? What drawbacks can it have?

_____

_____

_____

_____

_____

4. Where could I start expressing the positive aspect of this quality, emotion, or behavior in my life?

_____

_____

_____

_____

_____

INTENTION:

COMPASSION

1. Where in my life do I act like this, but I'm not able to see it? Where do I express this quality without realizing it? Where do I feel like this?

_____

_____

_____

_____

_____

_____

_____

2. What is the positive aspect of this quality, emotion, or behavior? What could be its benefit?

_____

_____

_____

_____

_____

_____

3. What is the negative aspect of this quality, emotion, or behavior? What drawbacks can it have?

_____

_____

_____

_____

_____

4. Where could I start expressing the positive aspect of this quality, emotion, or behavior in my life?

_____

_____

_____

_____

_____

_____

INTENTION:

ENDING

1. Where in my life do I act like this, but I'm not able to see it? Where do I express this quality without realizing it? Where do I feel like this?

_____

_____

_____

_____

_____

_____

2. What is the positive aspect of this quality, emotion, or behavior? What could be its benefit?

_____

_____

_____

_____

_____

3. What is the negative aspect of this quality, emotion, or behavior? What drawbacks can it have?

_____

_____

_____

_____

_____

4. Where could I start expressing the positive aspect of this quality, emotion, or behavior in my life?

_____

_____

_____

_____

_____

INTENTION:

BEGINNING

1. Where in my life do I act like this, but I'm not able to see it? Where do I express this quality without realizing it? Where do I feel like this?

_____

_____

_____

_____

_____

_____

2. What is the positive aspect of this quality, emotion, or behavior? What could be its benefit?

_____

_____

_____

_____

_____

_____

3. What is the negative aspect of this quality, emotion, or behavior? What drawbacks can it have?

_____

_____

_____

_____

_____

_____

4. Where could I start expressing the positive aspect of this quality, emotion, or behavior in my life?

_____

_____

_____

_____

_____

_____

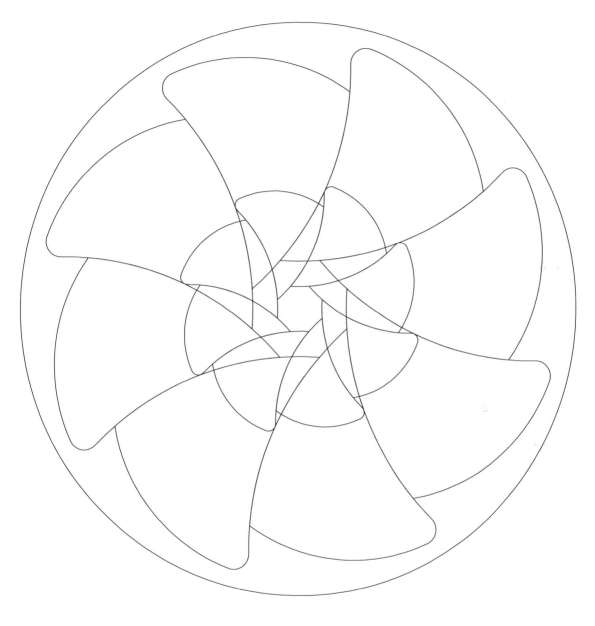

INTENTION:

About the authors

Lubica Hamarova

Lubica is a shadow work expert, coach, trainer, Zen monk, and pioneer in applying C.G. Jung's theories outside psychotherapy. She has been guiding people to change their lives, reach goals, and better connect with their inner self for more than 35 years. With a degree in clinical psychology and psychotherapy, she began her career as a university teacher, researcher, and psychotherapist, where she focused on psychotherapy and mental training for top athletes and how Zen meditation could improve their performance. Since 1992, as one of the first in Slovakia, Lubica has been leading trainings in emotional intelligence and personal development. She is the author of a special coaching approach and training programs that utilize the power of the unconscious mind to achieve tangible and long-lasting results. She has practiced Zen meditation for more than three decades.

Pavol Rozloznik (1957 - 2018)

Pavol was the "Creative Force" of Mandalive®, an expert on mandala design, graphic designer, guest professor, and Zen Monk. His fascination with mandalas started at university, where he studied fine arts. He was a multi-talented artist with a particular passion for graphic design. Among the best in his field, he was awarded the Identification Code of Slovakia prize for his lifetime work. His great love, however, beginning in his teens, was Zen Buddhism. In 1990, he travelled by himself to a Zen monastery in France and came back the first Zen-Buddhist monk in Slovakia. It is this unique combination of Zen mind and designer heart that made it possible for the Mandalive® mandalas to be born from his imagination.

Dana Dubravska

Dana is a shadow work expert, coach, and workshop leader who uses MARI (Mandala Assessment Research Instrument) in her coaching. She has a MSc. degree in psychology and neuroscience of mental health from King's College London and is currently pursuing MA in Jungian & Post-Jungian Studies at the University of Essex. Besides her adult clients, Dana uses the Mandalive® tool with children at elementary schools and special groups, e.g. children with Down syndrome, ASD, and intellectually gifted children and their parents. Prior to doing this work, she studied business administration and spent more than a decade in the fields of advertising, telecommunications, and logistics, leading teams of up to 100 employees. Dana has practiced Zen meditation for more than ten years.

Endnotes

1) Lind, A. B., Delmar, C., & Nielsen, K. (2014). Struggling in an emotional avoidance culture: a qualitative study of stress as a predisposing factor for somatoform disorders. Journal of psychosomatic research, 76(2), 94-98.

2) Rosenkranz, J. A., Venheim, E. R., & Padival, M. (2010). Chronic stress causes amygdala hyperexcitability in rodents. Biological psychiatry, 67(12), 1128-1136.

3) Understanding the stress response. Chronic activation of this survival mechanism impairs health. (2011, March). Retrieved July 11, 2017, from http://www.health.harvard.edu/staying-healthy/understanding-the-stress-response

4) Lieberman, M. D., Eisenberger, N. I., Crockett, M. J., Tom, S. M., Pfeifer, J. H., & Way, B. M. (2007). Putting feelings into words. Psychological science, 18(5), 421-428.

Printed in Great Britain
by Amazon